GRINGOS IN THE MIST

A NATURALIST'S JOURNEY
THROUGH ECUADOR

BY

GREG GORDON

FOR JANE GORDON
WORLD TRAVELER AND MOTHER

First Edition... 1995

laughing coyote press
669 Dearborn River Rd.
Cascade, MT 59421
copyright © 1995 by Greg Gordon

design & typeset by Arbor Vitae
printed on recycled paper by Mountain Moving Press

ACKNOWLEDGMENTS

Writing this book became much more an endeavor than I imagined. Withdrawn into myself, I spent countless hours in a small office at the University of Montana writing late into the night and developing a severe coffee addiction. However, *Gringos in the Mist* would never have been written without the help and support of many individuals. I'd like to thank Bill Kittredge for providing the original impetus and for his efforts to get it published, and likewise Gordon Kato at ICM for his suggestions. Ron Erickson and the Environmental Studies department at the University of Montana provided constant support, an office, and the Bertha Morton scholarship which enabled me to take the time to write. Roger Dunsmore, his red pencil, and Rick Freeman strengthened the work with their iron handed comments and editing. They also helped me learn to write as did Rick Bass and Terry Tempest Williams. I'd also like to thank the Rainforest Information Centre in Quito, Gerard Greweldinger, Britta Hanson, and the support and encouragement of my friends and community of Missoula, Montana. And thanks go to Jim Coefield for editing and layout. I'm especially indebted to Jeanie Alderson for her unflagging support and critique and pushing it in the direction needed.

Contents

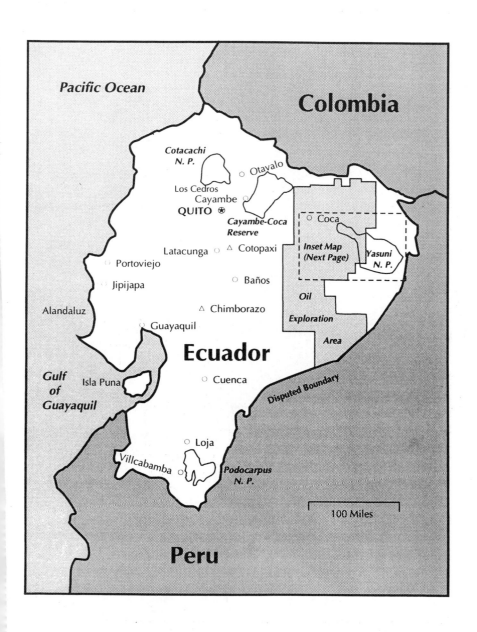

Pacific Ocean

Colombia

Cotacachi
N. P.

○ Otavalo

Los Cedros
Cayambe ○
QUITO ✷

Cayambe-Coca
Reserve

○ Coca

*Inset Map
(Next Page)*

*Yasuni
N. P.*

Latacunga ○ △ Cotopaxi

○ Portoviejo

Jipijapa

○ Baños

Oil

Alandaluz

△ Chimborazo

Exploration

○ Guayaquil

Area

Ecuador

Gulf
of
Guayaquil

Isla Puna

○ Cuenca

Disputed Boundary

○ Loja

Villcabamba ○

Podocarpus
N. P.

100 Miles

Peru

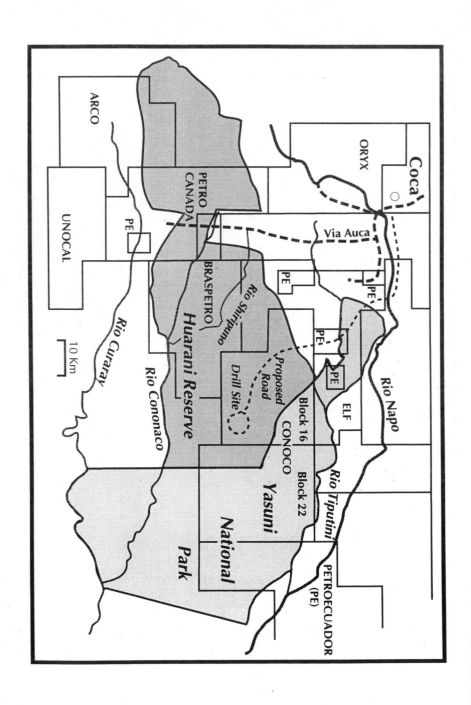

Only the Condemned is Saved

On the island of Martinique, too, a volcano explodes. As if splitting the world in two, the mountain Pelée coughs up a huge red cloud that covers the sky and falls, glowing, over the earth. In a wink the city of Saint Pierre is annihilated. Its thirty-four thousand inhabitants disappear—except one.

The survivor is Ludger Sylbaris, the only prisoner in the city. The walls of the jail had been made escape-proof.

—Eduardo Galeano

The naming of the world, which is an act of creation and re-creation, is not possible if it is not infused with love. —Paulo Freire

INTRODUCTION

> I don't like real experience. It's too hard to figure out. You
> never know what's going on. You don't have any control over
> events. I prefer to have life filtered through television. That
> way you know events have been packaged for your convenience.
> I like a narrative imposed on life, so everything proceeds logi-
> cally to a tidy conclusion.   —Calvin (of Calvin and Hobbes)

I suppose for many of us everyday life resembles TV a little too closely—
hyper-reality, the philosophers call it. In which case, fling open the doors
of unfiltered experience and turn your world upside down. Strip away the
accoutrements from your life—TV, stereo, friends, daily acquaintances, your
comfortable bed and comfortable politics and you find mirrors appear when
you least expect it, exposed to yourself, your experiences and your actions.
Our psyche is a cauldron that occasionally needs stirring to keep things
from sticking to the sides and bottom. Travelling, in addition to teaching
humility, stirs the pot and what surfaces often surprises us.

But a glimpse into the void was not what I had in mind when Gerard,
an old friend I hadn't seen in years, called me from upstate New York.

"What are you doing this spring?" he asked.

"I was thinking about taking some time off, getting tired of school," I
said absentmindedly.

"Want to go to Bolivia?"

"Sure." I looked out the window at the December drizzle. "Um, where
exactly is Bolivia?"

"It's between Peru and Chile."

"Oh, right." A glop of slushy snow slid off the roof and plopped on the porch.

"There's lots of big mountains to climb, 20,000 foot peaks," Gerard said, knowing just how to tempt me.

"No shit?"

"Yeah, I've been reading all about it."

"Twenty thousand feet, wow!

"Wah—the Chinese word for "unity," he corrected me.

"Wah, right. Twenty thousand feet. Jesus Christ! I've never been that high."

"So you want to go?" he asked.

"Sure. Why not?"

"And it's really cheap," Gerard added.

"Even better."

"Bolivia? Isn't that where Butch Cassidy and the Sundance Kid died?" I asked.

"And Che Guevara," said Gerard.

"Who?"

High mountains and steamy jungles captured my imagination for the next few months; maybe it was all those years of National Geographic. I told all my friends I was going to South America, at first just to see how it sounded, then to tell myself that's what I was really doing. It worked.

Suddenly, I had this compelling urge to travel, to experience the unknown. Does travelling fill a psychological need? Did I somehow sense my life had become static and was I seeking a radical shift out of complacency, or was I just trying to acquire—see who can go the most places, see the most Indians?

I suppose we all have a fascination for the exotic, after all, tourism is the world's largest industry. But what happens when we exoticize a place, a culture? In what way do we otherize, separate and isolate ourselves from our experience? Has tourism become another form of exploitation and colonialism we thought we left behind in history textbooks?

I wasn't thinking about any of this, however, when I met Gerard in Miami, and we boarded the plane to Quito, Ecuador, where we would stopover for four weeks before continuing on to Peru and Bolivia.

About the size of Colorado, and with ten million people, Ecuador is the most densely populated country in Latin America. From the dry Pacific coast the land buckles upward forming two parallel mountain chains with numerous peaks soaring above 20,000 feet, then plummets down to the Amazon basin. Running north and south, more or less continuously between the *cordilleras,* lies a valley 8000 feet high and less than thirty miles wide. *Nudos* or knots of hills divide the valley into links. Most of Ecuador's population lives here, with the exception of Guayaquil on the coast.

Before leaving the United States, it was necessary to get shots for a host of tropical diseases. The University of Montana Health Service had no information for traveling to South America so they sent me to the County Health Department where the nurse and I looked through the huge loose leaf notebook to find out all the diseases I would get. I received shots for yellow fever, hepatitis, tetanus, capsules for typhoid, and fat red tablets for malaria. The most widespread disease, however, was cholera, for which there was no effective immunization. Consequently, few *Norteamericanos* were traveling to South America, that year.

Until 1991 it was thought cholera had been eradicated in the Western Hemisphere. Yet we arrived in the midst of South America's largest cholera epidemic in history. The poorest countries were the hardest hit, Columbia, Brazil, Bolivia, Ecuador, and especially Peru with over 159,000 reported cases. Every day the Ecuadorian newspapers tallied the toll, "130 cases in Riobamba, 220 cases in Esmeraldes, 350 in Imbabura." By May, Ecuador had over 4000 cases of cholera leaving one hundred dead. In South America, 1200 died in the few months since the outbreak. It's estimated that cholera will leave 40,000 dead in the next three years as the epidemic spreads.

Cholera has been called "the world's stupidest disease." We know what causes cholera, how to cure it, and most importantly, how to prevent it, yet hundreds of people die from it. Human contamination of drinking water, caused by unsanitary and crowded conditions, induces cholera to spread rapidly. Cholera causes violent diarrhea and dehydration. The cure is simple: spend a week on a cot with a hole cut in the bottom and drink lots of uncontaminated water; for severe cases, intravenous saline solutions are necessary. Unfortunately, the ones who die, the campesino children, live far from medical help and their parents don't understand that the water carries the disease. In emergency measures, the government prints posters telling everyone to boil their water. However, it neglects to build outhouses. As cholera advances from the hinterlands, it also spreads in Ecuador's largest city, Guayaquil, simply because it lacks trash removal.

Lima, Peru, dumps 97% of its raw sewage into the Pacific. The cholera bacteria concentrates in the tissues of shellfish, one of the dietary staples of the coast. Twenty years ago, one of Peru's presidents received millions of dollars in foreign aid to build municipal sewage systems. He spent the money building a monument to himself.

Traveling was not as romantic as I had envisioned; most of it was dreary. The cramped rides in buses made for people five-foot-four, the asphyxiating mass of people crowding the marketplace, half of them aiming for your wallet, wore on my nerves. Smells, tastes, textures, and bowel movements never before experienced created an intense emotional upswelling which can never be replicated by "virtual reality."

Like all travelers I went through a period of culture shock. It's a very real thing. Distractions vanished and suddenly I was faced with day to day existence. I had taken numerous short trips to Mexico, but Ecuador was really the *Third World*. The poverty distressed me, but not as much as the realization that I was a part of the problem. I knew this intellectually, but it took a three month immersion for it to soak in on an emotional level.

I made a point of travelling light. However, cultural baggage isn't something you can lose at the airport. I had no idea how much my life-style and government policies directly affected the lives of people all over the planet, but the illiterate campesino who grows bananas and coffee instead of food crops knew. The Huaorani hunter deep in the rainforest whose only contact with the outside world is American oil workers knew. By being a tourist, by remaining outside, how was I responsible for such conditions?

I realized my own search for purpose, my desire to scale peaks, my preoccupation with pinnacleness, of getting to the top, was a form of machismo and was somehow linked to the oppression of others. Eventually I discovered the beauty of not climbing every mountain.

At what point do we cease to be spectators and become participants in the world? I began to understand that I wasn't an isolated entity, but rather a witness to the unraveling of the whole. At least I could find out more of what was happening, and thus armed with knowledge, I could do something. Not that I was going to personally save the rainforest, but by taking action I could save myself.

In a land where Che is second only in popularity to Jesus, I could not help gaining some understanding of who he was and what he was fighting for. On buses and in homes the faces of Che and Jesus are displayed side by side. In North America we have folk heroes, like Davy Crockett and John Henry. In Latin America they have martyrs.

And here I was, the embodiment of oppression—a white, middle-class American male staring at the faces of Jesus and Che as the bus hurtled down the Avenue of the Volcanos.

Quito and Coca

Excursions to an Auca Indian tribe can be made on Wednesday or Thursday from Quito. The limit of the jungle aircraft restricts the size of the group to 15. Observe Auca daily activities. Watch them cook meals over an open fire, weave, and make darts with which to hunt birds and monkeys. —*Flying Colors,* Braniff Airlines in-flight magazine.

The guide books recommend the Gran Casino Hotel as a good budget hotel in quaint Old Town Quito. Designated a U.N. World Heritage site because of its colonial architecture, narrow cobblestone streets, Gothic cathedrals, and open air plazas, Old Town retains much of its colonial charm, say the books.

"*El Gran Casino Hotel?*" I ask the taxi driver at the airport. "*Cuanto cuesta?*"

"*Diez dollares.*"

"*No? Es mucho?*"

"*Sí, pero es muy lejos.*"

"*Sí, pero dies dollares?*"

"*Okay. Ocho dollares.*"

I shake my head. He opens the trunk and reaches hurriedly for our bags.

"*Seis,*" he says, "*Cuatro,*" I say.

Gerard signals another taxi.

"*Cuatro dollares para ir al Gran Casino?*"

"*Sí, sí,*" He hurries us over to his cab.

Later I found out a taxi from the airport costs under a dollar. Ripped off on our first day.

"El Gran Casino esta en un lugar muy peligroso," the taxi driver says. *"No salgan en la noche. Es muy peligroso."* He makes a slash across his throat.

It's nearly eleven p.m. I consider going somewhere else, but where? No doubt this guy will take us to some expensive hotel downtown.

As he unloads our packs he reiterates his warning about it being dangerous and not to leave the hotel after dark. Looking down the narrow maze of streets below decaying stone buildings, I have to admit the neighborhood does look a little foreboding.

We are awakened from our sagging beds by singing in the streets at five a.m. At daybreak school kids fill the street. Diesel fumes perfume the morning air.

Over 40 years ago, novelist Christopher Isherwood traveled through Ecuador; he wrote:

> That is the irony of travel. You spend your boyhood dreaming of a magic, impossible distant day when you will cross the Equator, when your eyes will behold Quito. And then, in the slow prosaic process of life, that day undramatically dawns— and finds you sleepy, hungry and dull. The Equator is just another valley; you aren't sure which and you don't much care. Quito is just another railroad station, with fuss about baggage and taxis and tips. And the only comforting reality, amidst all this picturesque noisy strangeness, is to find a clean pension run by Czech refugees and sit down in a cozy Central European parlor to a lunch of well-cooked Wiener Schnitzel.

Well, we don't find any Czechs or Wiener Schnitzel, however we do find a refuge in this hectic city at the South American Explorers Club which is not nearly as neocolonial as it sounds. Run by two intelligent and beautiful women, Seriose with a Irish accent and Xanthe, from Canada, the pleasant house functions as a clearing house for climbing, backpacking and adventurous tourism. Seriose offers us a cup of tea, comfortable chairs, a library full of big picture books, a stack of maps, and a file cabinet full of climbing information.

When looking at a map of Ecuador the first thing you notice is the eastern boundary, or the lack thereof. Since 1740 Ecuador and Peru have been locked in a border conflict which occasionally erupts in a series of skirmishes. In 1887 negotiations began to settle the dispute with King

Alfonso of Spain as arbitrator. However, the claims were so convoluted that no decision was reached. Finally in 1942, eager to establish peace in the region, Brazil, Columbia, Peru and the United States signed the Protocol of Rio de Janeiro in favor of Peru. Not parley to this decision, Ecuador refuses to acknowledge the eastern half of the country as Peru. Ecuadorian maps include the east with a nod to the "disputed" border, which cuts through the upper Amazon and still has not been delineated. Outside Ecuador, however, the maps clearly show one boundary, that of the 1942 agreement. This loss of nearly half the country is a perennial political cause. Numerous politicians trumpeting national sentiment promise to take back the disputed area.

Overwhelmed on our second day in Latin America we try to decide whether to go north or south from Quito before heading to Bolivia in four weeks, when we meet Nicola and Brigid, from New Zealand. The Kiwis are keen on getting a group together for a jungle trip and need two more people. Quite a splurge, way beyond our budget, but it is the jungle. Gerard expresses concern that he hasn't begun taking his malaria tablets. The Kiwis introduce us to the fifth member of the expedition, Philippe, a rather abrasive French fellow on a whirlwind, four-month tour of South America.

"Gerard? Is that a French name?" asks Philippe.

We make plans to buy airplane tickets to the frontier town of Coca at the edge of the Oriente (Ecuador's Amazonia). When the travel agent says the flight is full, Philippe, fluent and forceful, says we've already paid for the tour, and somehow she finds five available seats.

After siesta we journey across town to the house of the guide's sister to pay our deposit. She shows us pictures and tells us about the trip in very rapid Spanish while Nicola and Brigid ("That's French too, no?" asks Philippe.) keep asking me what they are saying. Dealing with two languages becomes too much for my beer slogged brain.

I joke about Jim wrestling the giant anaconda but get "What's that?" from three people unfamiliar with Mutual of Omaha. We have a bit of a problem with sleeping conditions since the Kiwis want to know if there will be blankets and neither Philippe nor I know the word for blanket in Spanish. The woman assures us that "All is provided for—beds and plastic tarps."

"Yes, but are there blankets?" persists Nicola.

"Don't worry, all is provided for."

Nicola asks, "Will we get wit in the canoe."

Philippe and I both look at her.

"Wit. Will we get wit?"

A mocha river snakes through the vast greenness below as our plane descends from the clouds. As we approach Coca, roads divide the greenery into squares of banana plantations. Stepping off the plane is like stepping into a greenhouse; the air, heavy and rotting, drips from my clothes. A soldier in camouflage walks by. A green parrot rides on his shoulder.

Half a dozen other Americans, oil workers from Texas, disembark with us. Their fellow workers give us a ride into town. We learn that oil exploration has been going on here since 1970. The men spend two months here and return home for a month off. That night over more than a few beers, the exploration crew chief, a large, likeable man, with a gentle manner, tells us the oil company reforests the exploration sites.

"You can't even tell they were ever there," he says. I want to believe him.

They drop us off at the Hotel Auca, one of two hotels in Coca. The other is the Hotel Oasis, this one is supposed to be much nicer. *Auca*, a Quichua word, means "savage" which is what the Huaorani Indians were called until they were "discovered" in the 1950's. Ecuadorians still refer to the Huaorani derogatorily as "Aucas."

The Hotel Auca consists of two clapboard buildings divided into several rooms. A small padlock adorns each doorway. We drop our packs on the small sagging beds. Each building comes equipped with a bathroom, complete with a mirror and sink, paint peeling off the ceiling, a moldy shower with ants exploring the cracks, and a toilet without a seat or toilet paper. With our key we are issued a towel and a roll of toilet paper.

Bathrooms in Ecuador are often an adventure. Toilet paper is considered a luxury, so it's advisable to always carry a roll of the flimsy, blue tissue everywhere. Ecuador's plumbing can't handle toilet paper, so you throw it in a basket, if one is provided. I often forget; old habits are hard to break. But what I can't figure out is: What happened to all the toilet seats? Do they cost extra?

In one small restaurant I asked to use the *servicos;* the waitress waved her hand toward the kitchen. I walked through the kitchen, which also served the household, out the back door, through the courtyard with chickens and pigs, and there it was—a porcelain fixture on the side of the courtyard. At least there was a view.

Coca has two roads, both dirt, or rather mud, as it constantly rains, leading through squat houses with corrugated tin roofs. Mud mixes with oil making walking perilous. Most people go barefoot or wear rubber irrigation boots.

We decide to go for a walk. Crossing town takes no time and soon we are on the bridge across the Rio Napo. Skinny dugout canoes powered by outboards cruise the huge, dark river.

The first gringo to see the Napo River was Gonzalo Pizarro, governor of Quito and brother of Francisco, the conquistador of the Incas. In 1540 rumors surfaced of lands to the east rich in spices and the lost gold of the Incas. The Spanish found little gold in Quito and reasoned that it all must have been hidden somewhere. The highland Indians obliged them with tales of El Dorado to the east. So with 350 Spanish and 4000 Indians Gonzalo left Quito.

After what could only have been a wretched journey in Spanish armor over the cold Andes and down to the humid jungle, they arrived at the Rio Napo amidst torrential rains. The Spanish found no spices of any quantity, so the search for gold continued. Gonzalo commanded the remaining troops to build a ship to take them downriver. During the six months it probably took to build, many died of hunger, disease, and attacks by "savages," and most of the Indians deserted. Gonzalo sent his chief lieutenant, Francisco de Orellana, and a small party to float the Napo to the Rio Coco, find food and return. Arriving at the junction, Orellana found little. The river was much swifter than they thought, and they could not return upstream, so Orellana decided to continue downstream and became the first European to see the Amazon.

Floating down the Amazon, the expedition encountered numerous tribes. They fought with many and replenished their food stocks from defeated Indians. They also received report after report of tribes rich in gold and silver, always inland. Orellana, however, was more concerned with survival and acquiring food for the journey and let these rumors pass.

The chronicler of Orellana's expedition, the priest Cristobal de Acuña wrote, "These nations are so near each other that from the last villages of one they hear the people of the other at work." Within 150 years all of these nations along the Amazon floodplain had disappeared. Historians estimate that there were over ten million Indians in Amazonia at the time of Columbus. Now their population has dropped to below 200,000.

More than halfway down the Amazon, the Spanish were attacked by a fierce tribe led by tall, white women which Orellana referred to as *las amazonas*. An Indian informant told Orellana the women lived inland in houses of stone, and the men were captives of nearby tribes whose only purpose was propagation. After the women became pregnant, they sent the men home. Male babies were killed at birth and the bodies sent back to the men. The women were rumored to have great stores of gold and silver.

Eight months after leaving Gonzalo, Orellana finally reached the mouth of the Amazon and set sail for Spain. Long assumed dead, the governor, meanwhile, arrived at the outskirts of Quito with one hundred exhausted, starving, and naked men remaining from the original expedition.

On the other side of the bridge, a path leads off the road into the jungle. Excited by the prospect of a small exploration, we slop through the rich, wet earth into the rainforest and are soon swallowed up. Sounds of insects replace the sounds of humans, leaves replace gravel, mossy tree trunks replace army trucks. Huge ants—nearly two inches long—parade down a tree trunk. Smaller leafcutter ants cross the path, heroically carrying bits of leaf. These ants leave chemical trails for others to follow and, in time, these trails become ant highways bare of any vegetation. According to John Kricher's *Neotropical Companion*, which I "borrowed" from the Explorer's Club, in Latin America there are about two hundred species of leafcutter ants, the world's only vegetarian ants. They don't eat the leaves, but chew up the leaf pieces kneading them into a spongy mass, which provides a growth medium for a fungus tended by the ants in underground gardens. The ants feed on the fungus. Over the millennium, the fungus has lost the ability to produce spores for reproduction, and thus relies upon the ants for propagation. The fungus has become so dependent upon the ants for survival, it is unable to feed itself, as it can no longer produce the enzymes to break down leaves. The ants provide for all. This fungus has truly been domesticated.

"Hey check this out, it's just like a documentary," I say bending down to the ants trooping across the path. But I find I'm alone. Everyone else has slogged back to the road. I sigh and trudge back too. Brigid has fallen down and is covered in black goo, much to Nicola's delight. She makes Brigid stand in the mud so she can take her picture.

At the edge of town, women wash clothes, men and women bathe, and kids splash and play in the river. It strikes me that everyone is dressed. I suppose in this world of public bathing and washing, some privacy must be maintained. Standing waist deep in the Rio Napo, people soap their underarms, chests and crotches, like they are taking a shower under their clothes. How does it feel having tourists watch you bathe and wash your clothes?

Nicola accompanies Brigid down to the river. The kids giggle at her mud splattered body. She steps gingerly into the knee deep water and splashes herself. Grinning, a man hands her a bar of soap. She looks puzzled. He tells her to immerse herself in the water and scrub with the soap and river water. Everyone laughs at the *gringa* who doesn't even know how to bathe.

For dinner we eat wild pig and *guante,* or paca, a large jungle rodent somewhere between a guinea pig and capybara, accompanied by a fried vegetable, that as Gerard says, "We can't even fathom." During our post dinner beers we are befriended by Juan Carlos, from Columbia. He tells us about stowing away on a freighter bound for Tampa. He hid in a tiny compartment for ten days. Since he knew he couldn't shit or piss or he would be discovered, he only ate one cracker and drank one glub of water each day. Arriving in Tampa he was found and deported. He says he'd still like to get to the United States.

About four in the morning, a rooster crows followed by the pop-pop-pop of machine guns, then a couple of explosions. It starts raining and all is quiet again.

At breakfast, a boy shows us a *chucha,* a baby coati, a animal like I've never seen. It has short coarse fur, five claws, a long, almost tubelike, snout, a ringed tail, and a mouth far back like a ferret. About the size of a three month kitten, the docile animal likes to be petted. It scurries across the table snuffling its sensitive nose, obviously the primary sense organ given its tiny bead eyes.

All morning we wait for Whymper Torres, our guide. We would be anxious to get underway, if not for the stifling heat. Instead we are nearly content to sit at the outdoor table under the umbrella drinking the big 650 ml bottles of beer and watching a man walk down the street with an anaconda draped around his neck.

Whymper finally shows up and all is not well. He explains that the new army colonel doesn't know him and won't give him a permit to travel down the Shiripuno River, a small river a day's drive from Coca. The Shiripuno, a tributary of the Cononaco River, winds through remote rainforest before joining the Curaray River and flowing into the Napo above Iquitos, Peru, several hundred miles downstream from Coca.

Whymper asks if we would mind going down the Napo to another river. The Napo, a significant branch of the upper Amazon, is a major corridor of petroleum activity and we wished to avoid it. Philippe lobbies for a trip as far from the Napo as possible. So, Philippe, Whymper and I return to the army base to petition the colonel.

When we pull up to the base the MP's won't let us in. Whymper pleads and they finally let us through. We run down to headquarters. A giant plaque with a snake and "Jungle Command" emblazoned on it adorns the wall of the hacienda that serves as HQ.

The MP at HQ tells us the colonel is at the airport. So we hurry back to the truck at the gate and just then the colonel pulls up. Whymper explains he is a guide and he's done this trip many times before *sin problema*. The colonel says Whymper doesn't have a guide license and can't go. Whymper says he went to Baños for the guide course, but got sick and didn't pick up his certification. The colonel tells us we can get a different guide, one that is authorized to go, and Whymper has to give us our money back. Philippe explains that Nicola needs to catch a plane from Quito next week, and we don't have time to find another guide.

They argue back and forth, the colonel sitting in his jeep, and Whymper begging puppy-eyed, hands on the door frame. I feel ashamed for this handsome, seemingly capable man at the mercy of Franco Junior behind aviator sunglasses. The colonel keeps shaking his head. Suddenly he consents, as quickly as he said no. He takes Whymper's ID saying he could take us, but that would be it until he produces his guide license.

"No" is the standard answer to any request in Ecuador, changing to "yes" at some unknown time following extensive pleading. I found it difficult to plead when someone said "no." I wasn't used to someone saying "no" just because they could. I took it at face value. However, I soon learned that aside from outright bribery, whining and pleading is the way to get things done. People love to hold what little power they temporarily have over you, especially if you're a gringo.

We are further delayed by Gerard's feet. Gerard wears size 13 shoe and the largest in Ecuador is 9 1/2. We pull boot after boot from Whymper's storeroom, which doubles as his son's bedroom, in a fruitless search for rubber boots for Gerard. Covering most of one wall is a life size poster of a well-endowed Sports Illustrated blond, her pinkie fingers poking into her lace underwear. She wears nothing else. And does it very well. I can't help staring at it. All over Ecuador, molded blonds draped over calendars and beer ads cover the walls of cafes, bus stations, stores, and homes.

It's not merely the sheer profusion of tightly exposed flesh that strikes me so much as the pervasiveness of my own culture's single physical standard. Ecuador exports bananas, coffee and oil to the United States, and we export arms and blonds. If this molded Nordic goddess forms this boy's ideal, what will happen when his illusion collides with reality? Will he forever covet blonds as a symbol of North America? Or is it just that the exotic is always becoming?

The poster stares back at me asking to what extent is this jungle adventure another exotic male fantasy.

Whymper's daughter pulls another boot out.

BENEATH THE CANOPY

The Myth of Pishtako

Some years ago a bizarre rumor spread throughout the Amazon basin, a tale still believed in many tribes. It is said the white men come to the selva with their gifts in order to capture the Indians, take them to secret places, and render them into oil which is used to power airplanes, motor boats and autos. So fueled, these craft return bearing more gifts, seeking more Indians. —Will Baker, *Backward.*

Attempting to get more light, two large trees on either side of the Shiripuno River spread their branches forming a monkey bridge. Squirrel monkeys, light tan with black faces, swing, bounce and pivot overhead, chattering at the boat as we slow for a better look. Pissing from the tree-tops, they keep an eye on the intruders.

Nests of the oriole-like Oropendolas sway like pendulous testicles from overhanging branches looking as if they may break and plop into the river. Oropendolas weave these strange nests on the farthest branches as protection against snakes, and often, to avoid monkey predation, they build them near bee and wasp nests, which bulge like giant goiters high in the forks of trees.

Oropendolas are also susceptible to brood parasitism by cowbirds. The cowbirds lay their eggs in oropendola nests for the oropendola parents to raise. The cowbird eggs hatch earlier than their hosts and thus grow faster and often crowd the host chick out of the nest. Vigilant parents will eject the cowbird eggs, except in the case of oropendolas.

Neal Smith of the Smithsonian Institution found that bott fly maggots are a major cause of death in oropendola chicks. However, oropendola nests with cowbird chicks are nine times less likely to have bott flies than those without cowbirds. Since the cowbirds hatch first and are aggressive, they pick the bott fly larvae off the oropendolas. Thus, oropendola chicks with cowbird nest mates have a much greater chance of survival than those without.

However, Smith also found that oropendola colonies near bee and wasp nests often reject cowbird eggs; the wasp and bees also keep bott flies at a minimum. Cowbird eggs in these colonies are similarly colored to those of the oropendolas, disguising the brood parasites. Cowbird eggs in oropendola nests which are prone to bott flies, however, lack coloration since they are unlikely to be ejected.

A black bird with a yellow breast, like a meadowlark, darts along the shore. Large, rich-black swallows with white breasts swoop and dive above the river snatching up the morning insects with a snap of their beaks. A ringed kingfisher skits along the banks looking for fish. It follows us downriver, alighting on a branch or log every few hundred meters. Violent purple flowers burst through the green. The sky starts to sprinkle again.

A helicopter drowns the squawks of parrots, the hum of insects, and even the drone of our outboard canoe. Oil derricks tower above the green rainforest canopy like skeletons of dead birds. Uprooted trees line the river bank, their pale mats of roots ripped out and exposed to the sky. Disillusioned, we hope to leave the ravages of oil exploration behind as we near Yasuni National Park in the heart of the Oriente.

A Huaorani family signals us as our dugout canoe cruises by one of the exploration camps. The Huaorani had no contact with the outside world until the arrival of missionaries in the 1950's. Since then an estimated 20,000 Huaorani have died from introduced diseases. Now their hunter/ gatherer life-style is further jeopardized by oil rigs, seismic exploration teams, helicopters, and roads which open the rainforest to a flood of colonists from the Andes. And tourists like ourselves.

The Huaorani indicate in halting Spanish and hand gestures that they want a ride upriver. Somehow Whymper makes it clear that we only have room for one. Awui, a boy of 15, or maybe 20, I can't really tell, makes an instant decision and climbs aboard.

In Huaorani there are no words for time, no word for day, hour, minute, year, and in the jungle where every day of the year is the same as the next, why should there be? We have to leave by 3:00 p.m. Thursday because Nicola needs to catch a plane back to New Zealand so she can be at work next Monday morning. Awui will wait downstream for his family until they show up.

Awui has nothing but a t-shirt and blue gym shorts, nothing else for a four day journey. What could he possibly need? The selva is his home. Our canoe, on the other hand, is loaded with clothes, cameras, notebooks, binoculars, trashy novels, cans of tuna, a rusty old rifle, sleeping pads, sheets for mosquito netting, flashlights, a bottle of wine, toothpaste, contact lens solution, and plastic bottles of Coke and Orange Fanta.

We have six languages for dinner that night. English, German, French, Spanish, Quichua, and Huaorani. Whymper's helpers, Jose and Colon, speak Quichua, the indigenous language of the Andes, and Spanish. Whymper speaks primarily Spanish and a little Quichua. Gerard's first language is German, and Philippe's is French. However, they, Nicola, Brigid and I all speak English. Philippe and I are the only gringos who speak Spanish. So, unfortunately dinner divides up among Spanish and English speakers, and Awui has no one to talk with.

"Awui seems rather shy, don't you think?" says Nicola.

"We're probably the first white people he's ever seen," points out Gerard.

"Do you suppose we should try to talk with him?" asks Brigid.

"I say, Awui, Awui, would you like to come eat with us?"

Awui stops eating for a minute and looks at her.

"He can't understand you Niki, dear," says Brigid.

"How do you suppose he feels about our being here?" asks Nicola.

We finish eating in silence.

Is there any difference to him between white tourists and oil exploration?

After dinner, Whymper shows us how to craft a ground cover by hacking palm fronds out of the jungle and laying them down, their fingers interlocked to shed the rainwater. Jose carves out the palm hearts, which we gobble down.

Tiny red ants produce painful stings, and I quickly exchange sandals for rubber boots. Awui is barefoot as always, although his feet are so wide I doubt he could wear shoes even if he wanted to. He seems rather unconcerned about the ants. Are his feet so tough the ants can't bite, or are ants just not a matter worthy of notice?

The Kiwis are clearly not impressed with the sleeping arrangements. There are no blankets. Whymper strings up sheets forming a canopy-like mosquito netting under a giant tarp. This pacifies the Kiwis somewhat. It's too hot for even a sheet anyway. I grouse a bit that I've forgotten a sleeping pad and have to sleep on the hard ground, but make do with some clothes. Philippe seems a bit irritated that Gerard has bedded down next to Brigid. Awui lies on the ground at the end of the tarp exposed—no blanket, no sheet, no pillow, no complaints.

Other than the ants, I'm surprised by the passivity of the insects. Everything in the selva seems shy. I never use bug juice, not even at night. Sure, there are plenty of insects, but they are never too bothersome or numerous. The few mosquitoes just carry malaria and yellow fever, that's all.

The rainforest is much more benign than I suspected. Colon presents me with a forest floor centipede, about eight inches long and as thick as my thumb, its smooth shell a glossy maroon. After a few minutes, it uncurls on my outstretched palm and hundreds of feet begin to move in groups of ten—ten tiny legs move forward, while the following ten move back in undulating ripples of motion. I set it back on the ground where it coils up in a tight armored spiral.

Dawn in the selva is very noisy. The whistles and chirps of birds, the loud drumming of a *carpentero* (a great name for the large, Pileated-like woodpeckers), and the droning of insects narrate the incessant greenery. Whymper hacks at the boat with a machete, carving out a better place to mount his new twenty-five horse Evinrude outboard. This is its maiden voyage, and he positively beams when pulling the starting cord and the motor starts on the first pull. New outboards are incredibly expensive and hard to get on the headwaters of the Amazon.

As I watch Whymper's dexterous handling of his machete, I begin to keep a list—101 uses for a machete.
    -hacking out a place for an outboard motor
    -fishing
    -digging a canal
    -chopping down bananas
    -a support when crossing rivers
    -opening a can of tuna
    -chopping onions
    -communication in jungle by banging against a tree
    -hacking a campsite out of the jungle
    -making tent poles
    -smoothing out the ground to sleep on
    -opening coconuts

-picking up a poison dart frog
-a spoon
-a pointing stick
-collect sap
-cut firewood
-whittling
-carving a violin
-as a weapon
-spreading coffee out to dry
-harvesting papayas, oranges, grenadillas
-hacking off a piece of meat hanging in the market
-cutting off a piece of sugar cane to chew on   while walking
-as a cattle prod
-a measuring stick
-weed garden
-tree planting

We ply the dark river in a forty foot dugout canoe. Ours is constructed while the Huaorani's are literally dug out of a single log from the trunk of the Choncho tree. Three people with a chainsaw spend twenty days making a dugout; making it by hand takes one hundred days. Other dugouts, much larger and made of metal, haul supplies and equipment to the oil camps.

Each bend in the river reveals banks thick with new types of vegetation. Palms burst forth in a cacophony of green, shoving the smaller leaf trees aside. One species of palm shoots straight up, its trunk exploding in stiff four, six, and eight way fronds. Other palms dip and rise in the slightest breeze, fanning imaginary wood nymphs. Low shrubs line another stretch. Thigh-thick lianas drop into the river from trees with huge spreading crowns, sucking the water up like fat straws. Other plants such as epiphytes (plants that grow on other plants) obtain water directly from the moisture laden air, needing no roots and growing in the crook of trees. If a plant can spend its entire life in the branches of a tree, it is the first to receive light in the ceaseless competition for sun. And in the tree tops, the pollinators—insects, birds and bats—are more common, while the wind blown seeds have a better chance of dispersal than on the calm rainforest floor.

One type of epiphyte, tank bromeliads, have evolved trough-like leaves, that funnel water to the plant, which can store up to two gallons of water. These tanks support their own ecosystem of small insects, algae, frogs, snails;

fallen debris supplies the nutrients. (One study found 250 animal species living in bromeliads.) A collection of these tank bromeliads can weigh hundreds of pounds, stressing the host tree and even breaking off branches. Some trees don't take kindly to these freeloaders and have evolved a smooth bark that prevents epiphytes from gaining a foothold. Others have scaly bark which flakes off. Some trees don't branch until they are sixty to seventy feet tall. However, these adaptations don't appear terribly successful as epiphytes sprout columns of red flowers everywhere.

Layers upon layers of plants form a mosaic of greenery in what is probably the most botanically diverse place on earth. This high biodiversity resulted from the Pleistocene era when much of the Amazon basin dried out. Isolated areas, such as the Napo River drainage, remained humid, serving as a biological refuge. Many species still remain in the area as remnants from the Pleistocene and are now found nowhere else. An estimated 9,000 to 18,000 plant species grow in the area of Yasuni National Park. Jaguars, tapirs, monkeys, fresh water dolphins, 120 other mammals, over 600 bird species, some 500 species of fish, 180 reptiles and amphibians, and over 100,000 insect species inhabit this rainforest wilderness. Biologists and botanists estimate hundreds more species remain undiscovered.

Whymper signals Jose to pull the boat over. He grabs a vine and bends it toward the boat. Orange, egg sized fruit dangle from the vine.

"*Grenadillas*" announces Whymper.

Peeling back the crusty skin reveals dozens of black seeds covered in slimy goo. The goo is deliciously sweet and a little sour next to the seed.

"It's kinda like drinking snot," says Brigid.

"Is this where grenadine comes from," asks Nicola.

It would make sense but grenadillas are a type of passionfruit.

Before lunch we go swimming after repeated reassurances that there are no piranhas, although Whymper relates a few piranha jokes that lose something in the translation. We are actually more worried about the orifice-seeking candiru fish, which we dub the sphincter fish. In reality, the tiny catfish only swims up one's penis. Then this unpleasant creature turns sideways and lodges itself in with the barbed spines on the side of its head. The only way to remove the needle-sized candiru is to have one's penis removed. (This would be much worse than merely being eaten alive by piranhas. One intrepid English explorer was so concerned he made himself a device from a cricket cup to protect against any unwelcome guests.) Apparently urine attracts the candiru, so if you don't piss in the water there's little risk.

Awui watches intently whenever we go for a swim. The Huaorani have no body hair. As strange as we find this, they must find it equally strange to see these huge (Gerard is 6' 4"), pasty white people covered with hair.

The sun is out in full force now, turning into a warmsleepy afternoon. Brigid basks on the bow. Philippe waves his socks in the wind. Jose and Colon doze in the stern. Grey angry clouds turn into towering cumulonimbus and thin wisps. Oriole-like Troupials line the green banks flashing orange and black. Flaunting undersides of black velvet, an eight-inch Blue Morphos butterfly dances in iridescent blue around the bow of the boat.

Butterflies, for all their beauty, can be quite tenacious. Just ask the passionflower. Passionflower plants are poisonous to most insects. However, Heliconid butterflies evolved the ability to tolerate these poisons so their larvae can feed on the leaves. In one of the delicate interrelationships of the rainforests, a specific species of butterfly can only tolerate the toxins of a specific species of passionflower. Passionflowers then evolve new toxins to discourage the butterfly larvae. This gives rise to numerous passionflower species and corresponding butterfly species.

Not only can the butterfly larvae tolerate the poisons, they turn it to their evolutionary advantage. The caterpillars accumulate the passionflower toxins in their tissues, and when they become adults the toxins give the Heliconid butterflies a nasty taste for any bird predators.

The passionflowers also produce nectar, attracting ants, bees, and wasps to protect their leaves against caterpillars. Some passionflowers produce a yellow glob which looks like Heliconid egg clusters, thus "tricking" the female butterfly since she will not lay eggs on a plant that already has an egg cluster, presumably to reduce competition. Other passionflowers mimic the leaves of nearby plants as a camouflage against the Heliconid butterflies.

John Kricher in A Neotropical Companion, writes:

> For the time being, at least one passionflower species, *Passiflora adenopoda,* may have won the coevolutionary battle between insect and plant. Its leaves are covered by minute hooked spines called trichomes. Resembling a Hindu's bed of nails, trichomes impale the soft-skinned caterpillars. Once a caterpillar is stuck, it starves (Gilbert 1971). Does the future hold in store thick-skinned caterpillars? Time will tell.

A pair of *papagayos* flies overhead, squawking, their orange, yellow and red plumage spectacular through binoculars. These large macaws have a silhouette as distinctive and endearing as their Spanish name. *Papagayos* always fly in pairs and mate for life. If one dies, according to Whymper, the other searches mournfully through the forest, screeching and soon follows its partner, dying of a broken heart. Whymper places his hand over his heart and says, "*Es como yo y mi mujer.*"

The toucan is also a colorful romantic, tossing fruit to its mate with its oversized bill. Almost as long as its body, the toucan's bill is mostly hollow and thus lightweight. The huge bill is useful for clipping fruit from distant branches and eating insects, snakes and nestling birds. The male also uses its bill for fencing and aggressive displays. While the coloration might suggest a relation to parrots and macaws, the toucan is a member of woodpecker family. Because of a special "hinge" in their tail bone, toucans can fold their long tails up against their back, probably so they can sleep in tree cavities.

Whymper points to the thick vegetation lining the bank and cuts the engine. "*Escucha. Javelinas.*"

We hear a slight snuffling in the forest.

"*Son muy peligroso-las javelinas.*"

"What's he saying? What's he saying?" asks Nicola.

Somehow I've fallen into the role of group interpreter. I'm barely fluent in Spanish, and it requires my total concentration. Just as I'm getting the gist of what's being said, someone asks, "What's he saying?" Then I have to shift and think in English, summarizing what Whymper says. The Kiwis look at me as if to say, "I know you're not telling us everything he said because it took him fifteen minutes and you only said four minutes worth."

Gerard, however, is amazing. In just a few days he is able to understand a good bit of Spanish and gets tickled when he figures out how to <u>say</u> something in Spanish. A big grin spreads across his face and he shakes with the pleasure of communication.

However, even in a mutual language, pronunciations can be problematic. Gerard frowns when the Kiwis call him "Gered." They also pronounce the final "e" in Philippe so it sounds like "Philippe, hey?" It's not long before it becomes natural for everyone to say "Philippe hey." But he doesn't seem to mind. I think he enjoys this new twist on his name, especially when Brigid says it.

Whymper tells us the name Awui means "stick" in Huaorani, although he, Jose and Colon refer to him as "The Huaorani." As in "Take The Huaorani and clear out a camp site." Every evening our roles are clearly defined. The boat seats are removed for five of us to sit on while Jose, Colon and Awui set up camp and Whymper cooks. Clearly we are the paying tourists. We sit and eat around the makeshift lanterns while the others stand in the shadows.

"I think Awui is upset about something," Brigid says, and for the first time I notice he's not smiling.

"Really? What's wrong?" I ask. I've been so concerned about how he feels about our being here that I've failed to notice his daily concerns.

"Language is a virus from outer space." Who said that? William Burroughs maybe. The birds have a language, and the plants too. If it's so difficult just understanding members of our own species how can we possibly hope to communicate with other species?

In Huaorani, *wapumni* means "hello," "goodbye," "how are you?" and I think, "friend."

"Well, let's go then," Philippe says. He's been pushing for a hike through the jungle and this seemed like a good opportunity. We've spent four days travelling on the river, our campsites on small beaches. Our forays into the selva have been just a few steps, not much beyond the luminous strip of river. It can be rather frightening stepping into that dark chaos of green from the bright light of the known world.

"*Es muy peligroso,*" repeats Whymper.

"I'm not sure I like the idea of tromping through the jungle after a couple hundred wild pigs," says Gerard.

Javelinas, or peccaries, have been known to charge people, chasing them up a tree if encountered unexpectedly while rooting along the forest floor for roots, leaves, fruits and insects.

After another warning Whymper agrees. The selva isn't as dense as I expected—a vine here, whack with a machete, a palm frond there, whack, a small tree, whack. We soon became separated and lost in the neverending pattern of buttressed trees, vines, lianas, philodendrons, and green. Finally after repeated calling and wandering we all meet up again.

Whymper slices through a thick liana and cuts it into sections. Handing a piece to Brigid, he holds up one end of the liana. Water comes pouring out. Fresh water from lianas! Weary of four days of Coke and Orange Fanta, we greedily guzzle the sweet water. While vines are small and flexible, lianas are the steel cables of the plant world. Tarzan swung on lianas.

Awui stands back amongst the greenery, watching. Awui usually stands off to the side, quite reserved. Every once in a while he'll break into a wide grin, his lips pulled back revealing a mouth full of large broken and blackened teeth. Pain shoots down my jaw every time I see his big smile break free. Disease is unknown among the Huaorani except those introduced from outside. Their only ailment is extremely bad teeth as a result of a diet of fruit and soft foods rich in carbohydrates.

Awui doesn't seem thirsty. Some enterprising anthropologist determined (I don't know how) that the body cells of indigenous people require far less water than those of white people, which is why whites become dehydrated so easily. Not only is our skin color poorly adapted for sunlight, besides being hairy and overweight, even our very cells are squishy. We are basically Northern Europeans, physically adapted for comfortable, cloudy, places.

In *In the Rainforest,* Catherine Caufield writes that lower metabolic rates combined with a large body surface area in relation to bulk means that forest people sweat less and need less water. In a humid environment, sweating is an inefficient method of cooling.

Evidence also indicates other adaptations to forest life, such as the ability to store protein for several weeks, and the ability to thrive on low caloric intake and what we would consider nutritional deficiencies. We would be wise to explore these adaptations rather than insist upon Western nutritional standards for tribal peoples. Indeed, a UNESCO study stated, "Metabolic and degenerative diseases seem to be much more prolific in well-nourished communities."

We follow Whymper through the selva as he shows us various medicinal plants, explaining the uses of each one while I translate. We pass a tree with very phallic roots, almost lifelike, suspended about four feet from the ground. The roots grow toward the soil as the tree grows steadily taller. Or perhaps the strange bulbous root tips serve to gather moisture from the air.

Whymper gestures toward the roots. "*Las mujers Huaorani usan estos cuando se perdian sus esposos,*" he jokes in a low voice.

"What'd he say?" asks Nicola.

"Um, he um said, that this is what the Huaorani women use when they lose their husbands."

"Oh."

Whymper indicates a small tree alone in a patch devoid of any other vegetation. He points at small bulbs in the tree stems which house ants. The ants, which are fast and produce a very painful sting, attack any other insects or plants which stray within a thirty-inch radius of the tree. In return, the tree provides the ants with a carbohydrate rich nectar.

Back near the river, Whymper leads us to a large tree with a white trunk and big poplar type leaves.

"*Sangre de Drago. Es medicina, bueno por el estomago.*"

Well that's a good thing to know. It's also good for ulcers, skin lesions, cuts and bites, *todo*.

The rainforest is laden with medicines, poisons and stimulants, the majority of which the modern world is not even aware. One out of every four pharmaceutical drugs is derived from tropical plants. Many botanists believe the rainforest may hold the cures for cancer and AIDS.

These substances are often chemical toxins produced by plants to protect against unwelcome insects, herbivores, fungi, and pathogens. Noted ecologist Daniel Janzen states, "The world is not colored green to the herbivore's eyes, but rather is painted morphine, L-DOPA, calcium oxalate, cannabinol, caffeine, mustard oil, strychnine, rotenone, etc."

Whymper hacks into the trunk of the *Sangre de Drago* with a machete. He holds the machete against the tree so the black sap runs along the blade and drips into a red plastic cup. In the cup the sap, which is liquid and not very sticky, is actually a deep magenta. It dries purple on the blade, which I suppose would be the likely color of dragon's blood. I reach up and taste a drop. It's dryly bitter, almost poisonous tasting, I rub it on some insect bites; it turns white and soapy.

"*Es medicina,*" Whymper says.

Numerous hack marks from previous tours scar the tree trunk.

Late in the afternoon, Whymper signals Jose to cut the engine, and the boat coasts into a tiny inlet. Whymper stands on the bow hacking vines out of the way as we drift into the channel. Suddenly the narrow channel opens into a small lagoon. We startle five beautiful red and brown Archaeopteryx-like birds, the size of turkeys with head crests. Higher in the foliage I spot another dozen. The boat moves slowly. The birds don't flush but shuffle nervously about. These Hoatzins have great crests of feathers, and their faces are bare, with bright blue skin and red eyes. A Neotropical Companion says that Hoatzins feed exclusively on philodendron leaves, which they chew into a pulp that slowly ferments inside them, giving the birds an unpleasant odor and taste. But monkeys don't seem to mind, and often prey upon the birds.

Like the prehistoric "first bird," Archaeopteryx, young Hoatzins have wing claws that they lose when adults. They escape danger by dropping into the water; they swim and dive well. When the danger passes, the young use their wing claws to climb back onto the vegetation. According to biologists, the wing claws are coincidental, an example of convergent evolution. Convergent evolution occurs when different species have similar needs and evolve similar methods of dealing with those needs. This doesn't mean the species are related in any way.

However, I still prefer to think of the Hoatzin as an ancient species still surviving deep in the rainforest. And they do look like Archaeopteryx.

After watching Capuchin monkeys and setting up camp. Whymper, Philippe, Gerard and I head back out to the river to drop some fishing lines for the night. Jose, Colon and Awui fish for piranha in the lagoon. The Kiwis stay in camp.

When we return, Jose, Colon and Awui greet us with a couple dozen piranha, cleaned and frying in oil and salt.

"I think that boy may have a deficiency," says Nicola watching Colon empty half a carton of Morton's Salt into some frying bananas.

"Would you like my piranha?" asks Brigid holding out her plate. "I'm not terrible keen on it."

"Sure!" say Philippe, Gerard and I.

Although, fairly tasty, piranhas are very bony and not very big. It takes at least three to make a meal. Luckily, there are plenty of piranhas and banana chips to go around.

From the cleaned piranha carcasses, Whymper extracts the jaws, loops a fishing line through the bone and hangs a necklace of piranha mandibles around my neck.

Determined to see a caiman, the Amazonian crocodile, Philippe spends the evening down by the lagoon tossing a fishing line with a hunk of piranha into the water.

"He is out there. I know it," says Philippe. After an hour I grow bored and rejoin the others back at camp. Gerard writes in his journal. Nicola braids Brigid's hair. Jose and Colon wash dishes. Whymper fiddles with the tent. Awui stands on the bank intently watching Philippe fish for caiman.

Just as we crawl under the sheets which serve as mosquito netting, Philippe rouses me to take the canoe out to look for caiman. Silently we pole the canoe through the lagoon, while Whymper stands on the prow with my headlamp flashing across the black surface for the yellow glow of a caiman's eyes. Suddenly he plunges his hands into the water and comes up holding a five-foot caiman. Whymper apologizes that they don't get much bigger around here. Downstream, toward the Amazon, caimans grow ten to twelve feet long. For years Manaus, Brazil exported millions of caiman skins transformed into wallets, purses, belts, and boots.

We take the caiman back to show the others. Whymper places the reptile in Brigid's hands while Nicola takes flash photos. I don't really want a picture of myself holding a caiman. Lying limp in Brigid's arms, this creature hardly evokes fear, but rather pity and compassion. We carry it back to the lagoon and release it. The caiman slowly swims off a few meters and stares back at us, eyes shining suspended in the water, mysterious but not frightening. Whymper tells us about the Israelis he once brought in here who machine gunned all the wildlife. He will no longer take Israelis and allows no hunting on his trips.

The next morning when we pole the canoe out to the river to check our lines for fish, we discover the channel has dropped nearly a foot overnight, just enough to make getting through a major ordeal. The channel makes a sharp turn, and we manage to get the canoe firmly lodged, unable to go forward or backward. Whymper and Jose slice at the mudbanks with machetes to make a bigger channel. Gerard and I hop out and dig deep with wooden poles, prying mud loose from the bank. Soon up to our waists in mud and river, we all scoop up mud with our hands and slop it onto the bank.

"A shovel would be handy right about now," says Gerard.

Grunting and cursing in six languages we bulldoze the boat through. At the river, we check our fishing lines. Nothing.

For some reason, getting the boat back into the lagoon is even tougher. Finally at camp, we load a few things into the boat and carry the rest through the jungle to the river, while Whymper and Jose bring the canoe around through the massacred channel. The rest of us slide down the steep river bank into the canoe.

"It's so authentic," exclaims Nicola.

"Just like a movie," adds Brigid.

It is true that this is the first time we've actually done anything. We are sweating and coated with mud, actively engaged in the environment. Up to now it's been all scenery. Whymper and the boys indeed "provide for all." This is also the first time we've experienced any element of uncertainty.

Yet their comments trouble me. It reminds me we are on a ride, a Disneyland without cables. What is this sense of authenticity we seek from wilderness? As Jack Turner points out we've traded real experience for an abstract one. We aren't manipulating nature so much as manipulating our experience of it. No matter how "virtual" reality gets something will remain missing. Our wild animal nature recognizes that and seeks it out. Although the wild still flourishes (even Disneyland has mice) we've reduced our experience of it to nature shows, picture books and guided river trips, experiences which can be controlled and managed. This is ecotourism—a mad rush to see and experience the wild places before they disappear, driven by lack of authenticity in our own lives. Yet we are unwilling to strike out on our own. We require some degree of comfort, whether it be blankets or maps.

We head for the junction of the Cononaco and Tiguino, the river which flows from the lands of the Tagaeri. The Tagaeri, a tribe of the Huaorani, are one of the last uncontacted tribes in the world. Nobody knows how many Tagaeri remain. Estimates range from thirty to fifty. They are especially resistant to infringement upon their territory, and eagerly fire arrows and spears at any tourists or curiosity seekers, as well as oil workers. In 1987, the Tagaeri attacked a group of oil exploration workers who were laying seismic lines that cut through the Tagaeri gardens. The oil companies enlisted the help of the Catholic Bishop to missionize and "tame" the Tagaeri. Bearing gifts, the bishop and a nun flew into the area by helicopter. They were found a week later, ceremoniously killed with seventeen spears embedded in their bodies. And last February, eight Tagaeri were reported attacking a helicopter with spears.

We will turn around before entering the Tagaeri territory.

A beautiful scene greets us at the junction of the two rivers. We can see quite a ways in three directions, up the Tiguino where the Tagaeri live, and up and down the Cononaco. The selva sparkles with the recent rain. Thin clouds glow pink in the evening sun. The world lies quiet and peaceful as we sit on the gunwale of the dugout dangling our fishing lines over the edge. No poles. We just throw out a hook with a hunk of fish tied to a large monofilament line.

Three nights ago, Colon and I prowled the beach with a flashlight and machete. I shone the light right where the water meets the sand, while Colon peered intently into the water for a tiny minnow, machete poised above his head ready to make the strike. When we spotted a fish, down came the machete in the water sealing off any escape. Colon then used the machete to scrape the fish up on shore. With a handful a minnows as bait, Colon hooked about a two pounder. Whymper macheted it into bait, and the next day Colon caught a five pounder. Again Whymper hacked it into bait. Jose and Awui and Colon used some of the fish to catch the mess of piranha, and we're now using the rest as bait.

Whymper pulls slowly on the line; he's got something big. The fish pulls the canoe into the main channel of the river. It breaks the surface. It is huge—and then it's gone. A few minutes later he hooks another. When he finally pulls it up to the boat, it's a large catfish-looking thing. Whymper reaches out and stabs it with his machete, shoves his hand in the wound, and lifts it into the boat. It's about twenty pounds and three-feet long with thick leathery skin, a long sloping forehead, long thick whiskers and tiny eyes—not surprising given the muddiness of the river. It's sort of a cross between a catfish and a shark. I give its head a whack with an axe, which just bounces off its bony skull. I hit it harder and then try to kill it by severing its spinal cord with the axe and finally give up leaving it bleeding and gasping in the bottom of the boat. We make our way back upstream.

We have fried catfish and bananas for dinner, and the catfish soup the next night is delicious. This fish gives the eight of us three full meals. The piranha is tasty enough, but the catfish/shark is a true jungle delicacy.

That night Whymper tells us a few "ghost stories" of the spirits that live in the forest. The most common spirit is a "boom-boom," a deep drumming that comes from the trees.

"If you hear it, you be quiet and don't bother the spirits," he says.

Years ago, while on a hunting, trip a *compañero* ignored the folk warning and shouted back at the drumming. The drumming grew louder. The men shone their flashlights into the dark. Whymper's *compañero* panicked and fired his gun at the night. The booming moved closer and closer. They quickly wove crosses out of vines and twigs and placed them around camp to keep the spirits away, but the booming besieged them all night. By morning the disrespectful *compañero* had become very ill. They took him to a Huaorani *brujo* (medicine man or healer) who said the man was inhabited by "*espiritos malos*." He stayed with the *brujo* for six months, becoming very thin and almost died, but eventually recovered.

In a story reminiscent of many Native American myths, where the "keeper of the game" is encountered and dire consequences result from violating taboos, Whymper tells of hunting javelinas with five *compañeros*. They heard the javelinas and saw what they thought were two to three hundred of them moving through the *selva*. They could see the bushes move and had their guns out, but never actually saw one. So they split up. Whymper went to where he saw the movement and couldn't find any tracks, so he figured it was spirits. The others had already disappeared in search of the javelinas. He heard a couple shots and hurried off in that direction. He found his friend lying on the ground underneath a giant javelina which disappeared as soon as Whymper and the others arrived. This man came down with fever and could barely walk. They had to make a stretcher out of palm fronds to carry him out.

Another time, years ago on one of his first trips into the selva, Whymper saw a giant man walking the beach at night. He didn't approach the man, but snuck back to camp, never mentioning the incident to his *compañeros*.

Translating these stories with my mediocre Spanish and then writing them down a couple days later, I can imagine how difficult it must be to maintain any degree of accuracy in transcribing native myths. I'm sure part of me is looking for a point or purpose in the stories which will satisfy my own interpretations. Instead of just absorbing the stories, I tend to project meaning upon them. Often there is none I can discern. I can't tell how much cultural bias may creep in when I seize some sentences as important and gloss over others. In this shift from oral tradition to written, the text becomes "more real" or "more legitimate" than the original story. As language becomes validated through written texts, we begin to view the world as "The Book of Nature" to be interpreted instead of experienced, and perhaps losing the authenticity of the wild in the process.

We drop Awui at the Huaorani village and helicopter supply port. A large dugout-style barge unloads drilling pipe. Multicolored pools of oil float on the river's surface. The industrial smell of steel and petroleum mixes with the heavy green air of the jungle. A Huaorani family stands waving in front of two huge fuel tanks. Whymper hops off bearing animal crackers and saltines. Eight to ten Ecuadorians are also stationed here.

The Huaorani greet and absorb Awui, while I wander around the camp. An Ecuadorian *petrolero* from Esmaraldes, the petroleum shipping port on the coast, appoints himself tour guide. Standing on the cargo platform, he illustrates the helicopter loading procedure, holding a large steel cable above his head.

Standing in meek contrast to the loading crane, drilling pipe, fuel tanks, bags of concrete, and helicopter slings, is the Huaorani camp of wooden huts and palm roofs. A Huaorani man sits crossed-legged on his veranda next to a cooking fire and large black cauldron. Long, black hair dreadlocks down from his large head. He squints at us and picks his toenails. Four green macaws perch nearby; a couple of chickens dart about. The Huaorani men wear dark colored t-shirts and shorts, the women, long thin dresses. The children go naked except for fake pearl necklaces. Until a few years ago none of them wore clothes—quite practical given their hot, humid environment. One old fellow with the traditional distended split open earlobes, which form a loose loop hanging nearly to his shoulders, wears a yellow hard hat.

The rainforest is aptly named. It's rained on and off for the past three days. An occasional patch of blue allows the sun through until another grey cloud passes over. As we hum back up the Shiripuno, retracing our outward journey, the outboard breeze keeps the humid air moving past. Rafts of flotsam from last night's deluge float down the middle channel marking the swiftest current and making travel rather hazardous. Two-liter plastic bottles of Coke and Sprite, and plastic quart jugs of Castrol Oil bob in the logjams. Blue plastic fifty-five gallon drums drift along—escapees from the oil camps.

We head back upstream after an early morning swim. A beautiful Monday morning on our last day in the selva. Our destination camp—the beach where we spent the first night—is completely submerged. The rain of the past few days raised the water level about eight feet. We look for an alternative campsite, but the river overflows the banks. Water covers the forest floor. Poling the canoe among the trees, we finally find some high ground and hack a campsite out of the jungle. The next morning I notice one of the hacked lianas has sprouted a one centimeter core growth overnight.

Philippe motions Gerard and I away from camp. "Guys, guys come look at this."

"I shit here yesterday." He points at a lump of dirt.

"And look. It is gone!"

"Philippe, you lost your shit," says Gerard.

There was nothing left. It just vanished, carried off by dung beetles and other insects. The rest decomposed in a few hours. I look around the campsite. If Whymper brought each of his groups here, they would have to hack back the jungle each time. Everything is so busy growing, there's not even time to rot. Die, and the minute you hit the ground, bugs are making off with little pieces of flesh, and zoom, your bones decompose and are recycled into a mushroom or vine or philodendron shooting its way skyward. Sometimes vegetation doesn't hit the ground before the decomposers are at it. Once I hacked at what I thought was a liana; earth came showering down on me. A tree had decayed into dirt while still standing. It was supported by lianas which sapped nutrients as soon as they were released, in a self-suspended terrarium.

A small dugout sits by the shore of the banana plantation. As we pass Whymper shouts and whistles, then tells Jose to toss the remaining food—crackers and fish into the dugout.

"Esta gente es muy pobre," he says. Into the dugout goes a pack made of

woven palm fronds filled with crackers wrapped in plastic.

Well on his way to becoming one of Coca's wealthier citizens, Whymper wants to maintain good relations with everyone, colonels and Indians. Born in another place, Whymper would have made a superb politician; you can't help liking him.

I know of people who find Nature boring. I once lived on a remote island national park for a short time. One visitor exclaimed, "What ever do you DO here?"

Wilderness returns our senses to us. It takes four or five days just to flush the toxins of civilization from your system, but your senses stop filtering out all the noise, and you find yourself, not in a vacuum, but connected to everything going on around you. You become fully human again. You could die, you could get lost, you will be cold, hot and uncomfortable. Senses wide open, receiving, you suddenly return to civilization, and it overwhelms you.

I feel a sense of loss leaving the rainforest. I don't feel I'm taking something with me, so much as leaving something behind. I wish I could stay longer, perhaps float all the way down to the Amazon, like Orellana. These tapestries of a wet, green universe must do something to the psyche, and I feel my psyche needs something done to it.

However, even in the remote reaches of the upper Amazon wilderness is a facade behind which lie cartographic maps and satellite photos with oil wells sketched in.

The smell of oil fills the air as we near the *petrolero* camp where we picked up Awui five days earlier. The road following the pipeline back to Coca reeks of oil. Oil leaks from the pipeline into creeks and rivers. Swamps in the rainforest are covered in crude. For the past eighteen years this pipeline leaked over 16 million gallons of oil into the Oriente (the Exxon Valdez spill was 11 million gallons). From here the pipeline stretches 300 miles, climbing to nearly 10,000 feet over the Andes and dropping back down to the coast for refining and export (mostly to the United States).

I ask Whymper if the oil development helps the people of Coca. "*La gente? No.*" The workers all come from the United States or Quito, he says.

Even the road back to Coca is heavily oiled dirt. The rain turns it into a black slime waterslide. Trucks spin and slip on the thick oil. A long trailer can't make it up the hill, and the road is too narrow to pass without danger of sliding off the edge. Campesinos hack palms to place under the spinning wheels of the semi. Another truck doesn't make it, lies flipped on its side.

I sit on top of Whymper's open air "monkey bus" propped up against my pack. Clouds churn in the distance. At the top of a hill the rainforest stretches out for miles. Chickens peck and scratch at the road, their feet blackened by oil. Freshly washed clothes are spread out to dry across the black pipeline. Oil lies in pools in front of campesino homes while coffee dries ôn large concrete slabs nearby. School kids carry backpacks and wear yellow plastic raincoats emblazoned with the emblem of their donor, TEXACO. Oil plumes burn in the distance. As we get closer, a huge production facility comes into view.

The Condor Seeks a Wife

Each of us bears a unique relationship with landscape if we allow ourselves to let go—let go of the cultural biases and societal constraints, taking the time to experience earth as it is, raw and self-defined. We need to imagine ourselves flying on the backs of owls, for a people without a natural vision is a people without insight. We have the power to rethink our existence, our time in earth's embrace, and step forward with compassionate intelligence. If we align ourselves with the spirit of the place we will find humility infused with joy.
—Terry Tempest Williams

In Quito, Nicola catches her plane back to New Zealand; she has to return to work tomorrow, and Brigid continues her world tour flying off to Europe. I feel overwhelmed in Quito and need to escape the city. So many places to go; so many things to see. Cotopaxi, at 19,600 feet, the world's highest active volcano looms on the horizon. Anxious to get moving after sitting in a boat all week, Gerard, Philippe and I hop a bus to the village of Otavalo where we can acclimate and prepare to climb Cotopaxi, next on our list of "must do" things in Ecuador.

We meet Rodrigo Mora, a short man with a very neat and clipped style, both in appearance and speech, at "the tourist office," actually his apartment, where he sits us down and explains very patiently in meticulous Spanish the camping places around Otavalo. Lago Caricocha is his premier recommendation. *"Es muy lindo,"* he says kissing his thumb. Rodrigo rounds up a friend with a van to give us a ride up to the lake.

The driver of the van looks like a mafia chauffeur with a loose fitting grey suit and large handlebar mustache. I ask to stop at the gas station on the way out of town to buy some kerosene for my camp stove. The station attendant tells us you can only buy kerosene on Sunday at the market. Rodrigo takes us to another friend who he thinks may have some kerosene. This fuel shortage is puzzling. The guide books say kerosene is abundant as most people cook with it. However, Rodrigo assures us that most people have switched to propane in the past five years. "It's much cleaner," he adds. He disappears into a small house with my fuel bottle and emerges a short time later with it filled. That evening cooking in a cloud of black smoke, we discover why no one uses kerosene anymore.

The cobblestone road to the lake winds through hills cultivated with small farms of corn. Rodrigo tells us a family up here built this twelve kilometer road by hand. The kids brought in rocks while the fathers and uncles pounded the stones into place. The road climbs higher giving us an incredible view of Imbabura, a rocky plug of a peak. A heart shaped landslide on the mountain face, known as *El Corazon de Imbabura* seems to pulse in the pink evening light. Rodrigo calls this *la hora magical.* Across the valley Cotacachi's bald crown pokes through a halo of clouds at 16,000 feet.

Formed in the caldera of a not-so-ancient volcano, Lago Caricocha shimmers a deep blue. We set up camp while the last of the day's sun luminates the caldera rim. A nearly full moon shines brightly over the *paramo*, the high elevation grassland of the Andes. Under the moonlight, we climb the slope through waist high grasses to a rocky outcrop overlooking Otavalo. The outcrops and peaks stand in profile against the moon. The crater holds the moon captive and no light can break free from its dark waters. I could walk up here all night, but my bowels insist I return to camp.

In spite of my intestinal grumbling, the next morning we set out for a hike around the peak looming over the lake. Several hours later we reach the opposite side of the mountain. Cows graze below cutting trenches into the steep hillsides. Gravity and erosional slumping from the lack of ground cover pull the mountains toward the valley revealing rocky, brown earth beneath the grasses. Looking down at Quito spilling out of the valley, we realize this tiny island of paramo is spared only for the present by its altitude and remoteness from the mosaic of farms marching up the nearly vertical slopes.

Gerard and Philippe nestle in the tall clumps of grass out of the wind to take an after lunch nap. Lupines and hearty paintbrush add their blues and reds to the myriad yellow flowers of the grassy hillside. A strange plant, green and symmetrical, grows in bathtub sized mounds resembling a community of succulents. It appears as a single plant with many branches, each branch terminating in star shaped leafy buds.

The wind stops, and the sun breaks through the clouds. Two winged shapes lift from the rocky peak, hub of our horizon the past couple days. With one, two, three, ponderous flaps of their enormous wings, the birds are soaring.

High above and with white heads, they resemble bald eagles, only bigger. I settle into the grass and watch the shapes grow through the binoculars. From about a mile away, the white heads become white collar ruffs. This, combined with their ten foot long wing span and distinctive alula, that feather which sticks out of the farthest tip of the wing like a sore thumb, (actually it's the bird's first finger), characterize the birds as Andean Condors. The slot between the alula and the rest of the wing acts as an airfoil aiding in lift, much like a wing flap on an airplane, enabling the condor to soar at slow speeds without stalling.

Transfixed, I watch as the condors, the largest flying birds on earth, soar closer. I lay down on my back to watch them pass overhead. I pull the binoculars from my face. The condors fill the sky, not more than five meters above me. From their rocky perch miles away they had spotted us and came to investigate. Even with their bald head, that thick white ruff gives the condor an air of dignity their North American cousin, the Turkey Vulture will never have. What's in a name? Andean Condor and *Turkey Vulture*.

Condors, secure in their lofty perches, don't even bother to build nests, but simply lay their eggs on rock crags. Nesting near 20,000 feet above sea level, they often ride the currents down to the coast to feed on whale carcass.

The Incas appropriated the majesty of the condor making it one of their sacred symbols forming the eternal triumvirate along with Jaguar and Crocodile. The Indians of the *paramo* tell an ancient legend about the condor. John Bierhorst records a version in *Black Rainbow*:

The Condor Seeks a Wife

A condor fell in love with a young woman tending her flock of sheep. He changed himself into a handsome young man and came and stood beside her where her flock was grazing.

"What do you do here?" he asked.

"I graze my flock," she answered. "I sing songs, and with my slingshot

I chase away the fox who comes to eat my lambs and the great condor who tries to snatch me up in his talons."

"Would you like me to stay with you and help you chase the fox and scare away the condor?"

"Oh no," she replied, "for then I would lose my freedom. I love my sheep and I love to be free, to be alone, and to sing. I do not wish to marry."

"Then I will go. But you have not seen the last of me."

The next day the condor returned, again disguised as a young man.

"We can talk, can't we?" he said.

"Yes, we can talk," she said. "Tell me, where do you come from?"

"I come from the high mountaintops, close to the thunder," he said. "I see the first light of dawn and the last light of evening. And there among the brilliant snows I enjoy pure solitude and perfect silence. Won't you go there with me? You would be queen of the air. The clear blue sky would be our roof, and from the deep in the valley the flowers would send up their perfume. Won't you go there, my love?"

"No, I do not care for your mountaintops. I prefer my pasture and my sheep. And I love my mother. She would cry for me if I were gone."

"I will say no more," he said. "But do me one small favor. I have a burning itch behind my shoulder. Lend me the long pin from your shawl so I can scratch it."

The young woman lent him the pin, and when he had finished using it he went away.

The next day the young man returned.

"You have bewitched me," he said, "and I cannot live without you. Come away with me now."

"No I must not," she said. "My sheep would miss me. My mother would weep."

"Ah," he said suddenly, "I have the same burning itch behind my shoulder. If only you would rub it for me with your smooth fingers—smooth as alpaca wool—you would cure me forever."

As he bent over, the incautious young woman climbed onto his back. The moment he felt her resting on his shoulder he became a condor and flew swiftly into the sky with his precious cargo between his wings.

Higher and higher they rose, and after a soaring voyage they reached a cave near the summit of a mountain. In that cave lived the condor's mother, an ancient lady with faded plumage. And in other caves on the same peak lived other condors. A great multitude.

The condors greeted the young woman's arrival with shouts of joy and noisy flapping of their wings. The old mother was delighted to see her and anxiously cradled her in her huge wings, for she was shivering in the cold air.

The girl was happy with her young condor. He was affectionate.

But he brought her nothing to eat.

At last she said to him, "Your tender caresses make my heart happy. But I am growing weak with hunger. Don't forget that I must eat and drink. I need fire. I need meat. I need the good things that grow in the earth. I am hungry, my love, and thirsty."

The condor took flight. Discovering an untended kitchen, he stole some hot coals from the hearth and carried them home. With his beak he opened a spring in the mountainside and brought forth clear water. From the fields and pathways far below he collected bits of flesh from dead animals. He dug up gardens and brought home potatoes.

The meat was foul-smelling. The potatoes had gone soft. Nearly overcome with hunger, the young woman nevertheless devoured this unpleasant food.

She wished for bread, but the condor was unable to provide it.

All this while the young woman's mother was weeping in her empty house. The young woman herself began to feel homesick. She wearied of the bad food and the constant embraces of her amorous condor. She began to be thin and her body grew feathers. She laid eggs. She was indeed the condor's wife, the queen of the air. Hers was the work of hatching chicks that would someday soar fearlessly through the sky like their father.

And still her abandoned mother wept inconsolably in her house. Pitying her, a parrot who lived in the neighborhood came and spoke to her:

"Do not weep, dear woman. Your daughter is alive in the high mountains. She is the wife of the great condor. But if you will give me the corn in your garden and enough room in your trees to perch and nest, I will bring her back to you."

The mother accepted this offer. She gave the parrot her corn patch and room to nest in her trees.

The parrot flew to the high mountaintop. He chose a moment when the condors were off guard and picked up the young woman and carried her back to her mother's side. She was thin and ill-smelling from the poor food she had eaten. The glossy feathers that hung about her gave her the ridiculous air of an outcast human dressed up like a bird. But her mother received her gladly. She washed her body with the tears from her eyes. She dressed her in the finest clothes she had. Then she held her in her lap and gazed at her with boundless satisfaction.

Bereaved and angry over the loss he had suffered, the condor set out in search of the parrot. He found him in the garden, stuffed with corn, flitting contentedly from tree to tree.

He swooped down on the parrot and devoured him whole. But the parrot went straight through the condor's body and came out the other end. The condor swallowed him again, and again he came out. Furious, the condor seized the parrot, tore him to pieces with his sharp talons, and swallowed him piece by piece. But for each piece he swallowed, a pretty little parrot came out the other end. And this, they say, is the origin of the parrots we know today.

The sorrowful condor returned to his mountain. He dyed his plumage black as a sign of mourning. And the tears he left behind became the airborne ashes that swirl like butterflies above the hearth.

I do not feel qualified to interpret this story, for myths function as fictional truths. While one can perceive the mystery, the interpretation of that truth can cause problems. The interpretation, of course, is a result of one's own culture, attitudes, and beliefs.

This story does, however, echo North American mythologies in which interspecific marriages are common. "Salmon Boy" and "The Woman who Married a Bear," told by Indians in Alaska, also display kinship between humans and animals harkening back to the mythologic time, the dream time, when humans and animals inhabited the same world and could talk to each other. Unfortunately, the worlds have drifted too far apart and humans became sad parodies of the animal, unable to forget their human families and homes.

To seek aid in healing, only shamans, through elaborate ritual and psychoactive drugs, such as San Pedro and ayahuasca, are allowed to move back and forth between the animal and human realms, but cannot remain lest they become were-jaguars or some other malevolent spirit. Contrary to Western thought, Native beliefs indicate that animals are imbued with a soul and exist on equal footing with humans, both intellectually and morally. Indeed, many South American tribes believe souls of the dead reappear in birds.

However, this belief is not confined to South America. On the high Tibetan plateau, a sect of specially trained monks are authorized to perform a "sky burial." Tibet is too cold and dry for bodies to decompose, so the common burial is to be dumped into the river. However, a nobleman with enough prestige and money can request a "sky burial." In this sacred ritual, the monk lies the nobleman's body out on a stone slab and cuts it into small pieces to feed to the vultures. Soon the monk's yellow robes are covered in blood and he is surrounded by vultures. The process takes all day as the entire body is dismembered; the bones and skull crushed with a hammer small enough so the birds can swallow every last bit.

Lying on a bare hillside watching vultures, Robinson Jeffers wrote, shortly before he died:

That I was sorry to have disappointed him. To be eaten
    by that beak and become part of him, to share those
    wings and those eyes—
What a sublime end of one's body, what an enskyment;
    What a life after death.

I stand up, making it clear to the condors I wish to remain earthbound, for the time being, and they soar far out of sight.

Circumnavigating the peak, we come upon a lake far below. A dozen or so Quichua Indians gather tall reeds lining the edges of Lago Negro and lay them out to dry. The men chop the reeds; the boys pile them on reed boats and paddle the cargo to shore with long wooden double paddles— kayak like. The women take turns laying the reeds out to dry when not nursing babies. After drying, the long, light reeds are woven into sleeping mats. Many work barefoot and waist deep in the cold water, 12,000 feet above sea level.

This reed gathering event is as much as a social activity as it is work, since it only takes place these few days of every year when the reeds are ready to be harvested.

My daily bowel battle begins again. I need to stop every ten minutes or so on the way back to camp. At one point it even becomes difficult to walk. Gerard, who is planning on medical school, is concerned.

"Is it completely liquid?"

"Yeah," I groan.

"And how many days?"

"Three or four."

"Didn't you have the runs in the jungle?"

"Yeah, but that kinda cleared up after a couple days."

"If it's completely liquid, it's serious."

"I've been taking that Sangre de Drago but that hasn't been working too well, I may resort to modern medicine."

"And drink lots of water. Maybe you should see a doctor and make sure it's not cholera."

The hike down from Lago Caricocha to Otavalo the next day is quite pleasant, very pastoral. Fields of corn and cows grazing on the lush grass surround small whitewashed cottages with red tiled roofs. Rocky peaks tower above and my intestinal troubles seem under control. Nearing town, two boys run up to me. The older boy, Carlos, wants to try on my back-pack which is bigger than he. At first I think he's about seven, but Carlos says he's twelve. Nutritional deficiencies conspire to keep kids small. I hold the pack while he loops his arms through the straps. The pack hangs inches above the ground and the weight nearly pulls him backward. He takes the pack off shaking his head.

"*Que tienes en la mochilla?*" he asks.

"*Vamos a ver,*" I say and open the pack retrieving binoculars which of course are more fun if you look through them the wrong way.

I pull out some cheese and crackers, which seem like quite a treat, and we sit on the stone bridge eating and talking.

As I get ready to leave, Carlos gives me a bracelet he made.

Quichua women pass by dressed in traditional white billowy blouses, loops and loops of gold bead necklaces, and sweeping skirts of pleated green, blue, and magenta, and the ubiquitous derby hat. They carry bundles of sticks for firewood on their backs. Their smooth, dark skin, chiseled fea-tures, black hair and disarming smiles are striking. The white slacks of the men offset a long single braid down their back. I'm lost in an ancient Inca empire.

Hoisting my high-tech backpack pulls me back. How strange I must look, tall and disheveled. For a moment I feel self-conscious, but school is letting out for the siesta and all the kids say, "*Buenas dias,*" as they pass. I'm so obviously foreign that it doesn't matter.

Sweaters
and Organ Theft

The Culture of Terror

Blatant colonialism mutilates you without hiding: It prohibits you from speaking, from acting, from being. Invisible colonialism, on the other hand, convinces you that servitude is your destiny and impotency is your nature: it convinces you that you are not able to speak, not able to act, not able to be.
— Eduardo Galeano

We arrive at our hotel in Otavalo just in time for cocktail hour. The hotel courtyard serves as an afternoon gathering place. With rum at two dollars a bottle and a bottle of beer at fifty cents, both appear every afternoon as travelers swap stories and complain about the Ecuadorian music dribbling from the speakers, a monotonous latin disco beat with synthesized pan flutes.

Tropical diseases are always popular. Amoebas, trypanosomes, leishmaniasis, tapeworms, flukes, roundworms, malaria, yellow fever, typhoid fever, and hepatitis. One guy tells about a creature that lays eggs under your skin and the larva hatch into long, thin worms. The only way to get them out is to cut open your skin and pull them out like strands of spaghetti. Trina, from Germany, mentions brain worms, a parasite that eats brain cells. You can get them from eating unwashed strawberries. She says this fellow who got them was eating dinner with his friend who looked up from his meal and saw the worms moving across the whites of his friend's eyes.

And of course malaria, which has killed millions of people, remains widespread. In 1633 a Jesuit priest learned from the Indians, of a tree found in southern Ecuador which cured malaria. However, it wasn't until King Charles II was cured of malaria by a layman using bark of this cinchona tree that Europe acknowledged the discovery. Cinchona trees are rare, growing in the wet Andean highlands, and collection proved difficult for centuries. Finally in 1820, two French doctors distilled quinine (from the Indian name *quinaquina*— "bark of barks") from the cinchona bark.

The mosquitoes that carry malaria primarily dwell in the forest canopy, and with rapid deforestation and construction of reservoirs malaria is now on the increase. The disease is also proving resistant to quinine and synthetic quinine substitutes. Scientists are currently searching for new anti-malaria drugs, again by asking the indigenous people living in the forest.

Robberies are even more popular than tropical diseases, possibly because everyone has a robbery story, while not everyone has a tropical disease. Most are pickpocket stories, with a few armed robberies thrown in for spice. Kaes and Marti (a Dutch writer/photographer team reporting on development projects) often said how they never had a problem in five years traveling through Asia. On their second day in South America, they were robbed at knife point in Rio de Janeiro. They were appalled because the police didn't want to take a report as it was such a common occurrence. Marti climbed on the desk and refused to budge until they took a statement.

Over a few rum and Cokes, Jim, a traveler from Switzerland, tells about the best friend of his last traveling companion. While traveling through Peru, this friend met a young man on a bus who seemed like a nice guy. They began talking; the young man said he was a medical student. It was a long bus ride and at one point the med student offered the friend a Coke. Normally you wouldn't accept something from a total stranger in a foreign country, but the med student was well dressed and seemed like a nice guy and the friend didn't want to offend him, so he drank some of the Coke. Then next thing he knew he woke up in a hospital in Lima. The nurses said he was found in a back alley stitched up. He was missing a kidney.

Apparently kidneys bring a high price on the black market.

I've already been severely cautioned about anyone being overly friendly.

There are so many rip-off scams; like the paint or perfume scam where someone spills something on you and someone else insists on helping clean it off, cleaning you of your wallet as well. Pack and purse slashing is also common. But organ theft?

You can drink two kinds of beer in Ecuador—Club and Pilsner. Neither are great, but are surprisingly drinkable, and many a meal of rice and yuca can be salvaged with a couple bottles of Pilsner. Club comes in a regular twelve ounce bottle and costs about a dollar. Pilsner isn't quite as good, but it comes in a 650 ml bottle for half the price. So naturally everyone tries to sell Club, and everyone drinks Pilsner.

We grow weary of getting Club when asking for "*una cerveza*," and often we're told "*no hay*" to requests for Pilsner. At dinner that evening a boy tells us "*no hay*," there's only Club. We watch as he then opens the refrigerator and see rows of Pilsner. When he returns Philippe walks behind the counter and up to the refrigerator, flings the door and says, "*Sí, hay*." The boy laughs and gives us three cerveza grandes.

As extension of "*no hay*," one often hears, "*no hay cambio*," meaning "there is no change." In a country with 30% inflation, the largest currency denomination is a 5000 sucre note, about five dollars. So you walk around with a wad of 5000 and 1000 sucre notes. Consequently, if your bill is 2650 sucres, few people have 100 sucre bills, much less 50's. So often the merchant simply replies, "*no hay cambio*," or the occasional variation, "*no hay suelto*," Of course you have no choice but to let them keep the change. I have no problem with receiving 300 sucres as change for 2650, but the 100's start adding up when "*no hay cambio*," becomes too frequent. The honest merchant will give you a blank expression and hand back your 5000 saying, "*no hay cambio*," as way of apology implying that you should go dig up the proper amount and return. Most, however, are not above skinning a gringo for a few hundred sucres and take your large bill, put it in the cash drawer and feign surprise that you are still waiting for your change.

Philippe insists on getting the correct change. "They're always trying to rip you off," he tips us. At the bus station we're charged 1000 sucres for a 750 sucre ride. Philippe throws a fit at the girl behind the counter. The manager comes over, relents and charges us the proper fare. Philippe continues to berate the woman until she finally says forget it and refuses to sell him a ticket at any price.

"It's only a quarter," I say.

"It's the principle of the thing."

Gerard agrees saying, "It's Zen to be an asshole in a country full of assholes."

And if you become frustrated at all of this, a soothing phrase comes floating through the anger, *"No hay problema."*

At breakfast in the local diner, the old woman at the till miscalculates and overcharges us by thirty-five cents. Gerard insists she re-add the figures. This time she gives us back an extra seventy cents.

"Hey, it's not my fault these people can't even add," he says pocketing the extra money.

I oscillate between being embarrassed by fellow gringo penny pinchers and feeling indignant at being taken advantage of.

On Friday night the entire hotel is awakened by a drunk Italian yelling at full volume.

"Hey, we are brothers. Come with me. We must unite! German, Italian, Swiss, all Europe is brothers, why won't you be my brother?"

Apparently the Germans are ready for bed but the Italian still has a few drinks left in him.

"My brothers we must unite. Unity! It is Unity!"

"My brothers, I tell you we are brothers, why is Italy not a brother?" he cries.

I'm not sure if he's referring to the latest EEC conferences or cajoling them into more drinking.

"Come my brothers, tell me. We must have Unity!"

Receiving no answer he quiets for a moment.

"OK. OK!" he slams against the closed door. "Remember, remember Unity! Unity! and… alright then, FUCK YOU!"

Saturday is market day in Otavalo, perhaps the most famous market in South America. The place is packed with Otavaleños, Quichua, Ecuadorians and a smattering of gringos. Stalls in the market overflow with chickens, oranges, bananas, guinea pigs, limes, rice, corn, combs, sunglasses, blue cakes of soap stacked high, a zillion different kinds of beans and potatoes. And in the food court bubble huge tureens of *caldo*, usually chicken or beef broth with hunks of fat floating in it. You get a bone with your soup; sometimes it even has meat on it.

One minute you're in a crowded village market checking out all the stuff and the next minute, a guy bumps into you, a woman's purse flies up in your face, your body senses danger, your heart beats rapidly, you start sweating, adrenaline flows, and then you're alone with empty pockets.

He only gets about $1.50 but the whole experience depresses me. I retreat to a small patio cafe. It's such a small amount; people get pickpocketed all the time, I remind myself. This feeling of being violated, being taken advantage of and not being able to do anything about is so foreign to me. We gringos are so quick to jump to the defence, to run to the police insisting, "We will not be taken advantage of." There's nothing so awful as feeling helpless.

I think back on the fifty dollars that was stolen from my luggage during the flight from Quito to Coca. The flight was delayed for three hours in which time someone went through my pack and came across my wallet, empty except for credit card, driver's license and a fifty hidden inside. When I discovered my wallet in disarray in Coca, I went to the police station. Gerard and Philippe urged me to forget it; there was nothing to be done, which of course made me all the more determined to press my case. The lone policeman dutifully pecked out a report on an ancient typewriter. Back in Quito I presented the report to the president of Ecuatorina airlines, who shrugged and asked what I expected him to do about it.

After two or three cups of real coffee, a bowl of fruit and yogurt, and a healthy dose of self pity, I'm ready to venture back out into the main plaza laden with beautiful weavings, sweaters, hats, jewelry, shirts, handbags, carvings, everything for the buying tourist. But it is the sweaters for which Otavalo is famous.

The baggy, brightly colored wool sweaters with Guatemalan patterns and killer whales, obviously dictated by North American tastes, abound on college campuses throughout the United States. The indigenous people don't wear these sweaters; they wear thin, plain brown or gray Goodwill-type sweaters imported from Southeast Asia.

Because of the popularity of the sweaters, Otavaleños are the most well off indigenous people in Ecuador, perhaps all the Andes. Otavalo is a beautiful town, the people have done well for themselves; the streets are the cleanest in Ecuador. (Is this an American talking, or what?) Otavalo is held up as an example of a sustainable economy in the modern world. However, this success is built upon the exploitation of neighboring indigenous people, as we discover when Rodrigo Mora invites us on a behind the scenes tour of the sweater industry.

The ultimate source of the sweaters is the sun. Or rather Inti Raymi, the ancient Inca festival of the Sun. Rodrigo explains that Inti Raymi involves massive inebriation of a corn mash (chicha). The men go from house to house eating and drinking and dancing. The woman's job is to watch her husband, and when he falls down and passes out from too much celebration, take him home, until he wakes up and rejoins his group of revelers. This goes on for ten days or so; the end is rather arbitrary, probably when the alcohol is gone, or the women get tired of picking up their hubbies.

As the men dance, they chant and bump into each other. As the alcohol flows the bumping grows; the bumping gets more violent and slips into jabbing and hitting. Then the women begin to throw stones into the dancers until there is blood or someone dies. If blood flows it means the earth will produce a bountiful harvest next year. If someone dies without any blood, a bad year is in store.

The purpose of this fiesta (aside from getting plowed) is to thank the earth for her offerings and to ask for continued fertility.

A central part of the fiesta is a ritual bathing in which only the men take part. Apparently they're the ones in need of purification. The leaders of each group find a spring, or better, a waterfall, and the men bathe and dance and cleanse their souls before all the drinking starts.

Blood, martyrdom, and baptism seem to be universal rites, rather than adaptations to Christianity. In fact, the Inca religion included confession of sins and a convent system for "daughters of the sun" who couldn't have relations with men and lived communally. In one house we visit, the sole ornamentation is a picture of Jesus with an exposed heart, shot through with spears. In another house I notice a cross made of hair and reeds to ward off evil spirits. Ancient rituals and beliefs still flourish beneath the thin veneer of Christianity.

Inti Raymi is New Year's Eve, Thanksgiving, Halloween, Easter and Christmas (everyone gives and receives presents) all rolled into one with a more than thousand year tradition. It lasts from June 22, the summer solstice, to July and sometimes through August. It's not something you want to miss.

Because of the social and cultural importance of Inti Raymi, many of the impoverished villagers near Otavalo need money for the festival. This is gladly loaned by the merchants in Otavalo in exchange for future labor in the knitting of sweaters.

Sometime after the fiesta the merchant returns and says, "Hey, how about that money you owe me." The Quichua shrugs his shoulders and points at his corn field and pigs and says he has no money.

"No problem, here's some wool, make me some sweaters to pay off your debt," says the merchant. The rural Quichua and his family go to work knitting sweaters. Before he pays off the debt, the merchant, being a good, friendly sort, pops back by and asks if his new worker needs any money. The Quichua looks at his wilting corn and hungry kids clamoring for candy and nods. So the agent gives him some more money and some more wool.

The makers of the sweaters receive $1-6; the merchants sell the sweaters in the tightly controlled Otavalo market for $10-$15. These in turn fetch $40-$60 in the United States.

A number of people have figured out this indentured servitude and begun making their own sweaters, except they need to buy the wool which comes from the merchant. So they buy wool on credit and make sweaters to pay off the debt.

"Why don't the villagers sell their sweaters in Otavalo?" I ask Rodrigo.

He says the merchants "own" all the stalls in the market by paying the police to keep out the "nonmembers."

With this introduction, we walk into the village of Carabuela. It's raining lightly. Black and white blotched Holsteins graze in the shadow of the volcano, Mama Cotacachi.

Skeins of white and black wool dry on the hillside. A creek runs along the edge of the village where three women wash clothes, standing in the cold water beating them against a flat rock. The creek is not only the Laundromat and bathtub, but also the village's drinking supply.

High on the hill overlooking Carabuela sits a water tower. Empty. Built with foreign aid. Somehow the money ran out before the pumps and filter system were installed. This morning's paper announced 500 cases of cholera in Imbabura province. Rodrigo tells us there's a 30% infant mortality in these villages.

Gerard, Philippe, Kaes and Marti, and I are joined by two carloads of French families; one man is from the embassy and the other an engineer.

We walk up the muddy slope through the corn fields and along a mud wall, a foundation of an earlier house. In 1987 most of the villages near Otavalo were destroyed by an earthquake. The government, with foreign assistance, supplied grey cinder blocks for the people to rebuild their homes. While not as insulating as adobe, the cinder block is easier to build with. However, the cinder blocks make the village seem like a shanty town and look like poverty.

I wonder, can poverty only be defined in terms of income? Can people be made to feel impoverished by their surroundings?

Rounding the corner we enter a back courtyard. A pig rummages among discarded vegetables. A strong odor of wet barnyard animals, rotting vegetable matter and burnt bacon overwhelms the aftershave of the French engineer. A starving dog, teats hanging down from numerous litters, shivers in the rain. A small barefoot Quichua man comes out of the dark cube of the cinder block house. He lays out a reed mat and sets down a bucket of wool. He begins to card the wool, cleaning it using stiff wire brushes. Carding the wool is a simple job and is often done by children, even though breathing the fiber filled air is hazardous.

A little girl with a dirty face, barefoot and in worn clothes stands in the mud clutching a house beam. Japanese video cameras hand held by French diplomats whirl and click.

Next we visit a woman who spins the carded wool on a large rickety spinning wheel, not much resemblance to the works of art spinning wheels of Europe. The spindle is a metal bar and the wheel is a large wooden hoop, more or less circular. Other spinning wheels use bicycle wheels. The woman smiles a toothless grin. Her little girls sit in a pile of corn nearby. The French girl parcels out a handful of candy in each of their laps.

The Quichua girls sit in the corn, sucking sweets. A telephoto autofocus murmurs electrically from under a Patagonia raincoat. Taking a couple pictures myself, I feel an uneasiness in my gut.

That's where it hits, the poverty, the exploitation, the tossing of candy to kids screaming after each piece. Not in the heart. Not in the brain. A swallow doesn't help. It's not like a hunger pain; it's not like a stomach cramp. It's more like that feeling ten minutes after someone punches you in the stomach. Only it's not in the stomach, but in the abdomen, right behind the belly button.

We enter another house where children knit the spun wool like madmen. They produce one sweater per day. The house is cinder block, twelve feet by five feet. Cooking is done over a stone fireplace heated with wood. An ocelot skin, a certificate from the institute of wool dying, and pictures cut from old magazines—characters from the movie Star Wars—decorate the wall. The only furniture is a table and a few chairs. Half a bottle of orange Fanta sits on the table next to a small black and white TV. A colored piece of plastic is taped over the screen transforming it into color television.

What happens when they watch Dallas on television? Or see strangers with movie cameras wearing sweaters they made? Is this another form of oppression, dangling in front of somebody something they can never have?

As we leave, a teenage girl stands outside wrapped in a towel washing her hair under a hose. Everyone snaps a photo. How does it feel to have your life-style on display, to be a quaint photo? What possesses us to take a picture of someone taking a shower? What happens when someone becomes a photo subject, part of a collection of objects to remember Ecuador? It seems that a loss of dignity, a loss of humanity results for both collected and collector. But isn't that what we're all doing here—collecting images, memories, experiences, objects? We ignore the essence and take photos to preserve images locked in time and space. The brilliant Blue Morphos butterflies fade as soon as they are killed and mounted.

The next stop is the co-op. Beautiful sweaters hang along the wall. The few artisan co-ops attempt to address the problem of exploitation, but aren't overly successful. They can't pay the workers until the goods are sold, whereas the merchants can pay right away or even before the sweater is finished. And how does one know if you're buying from a co-op in an Andean village when shopping in Berkeley?

An old man demonstrates a backstrap loom attached to the wall. He sits on the dirt floor strapped to the loom. To get a tight weave he must yank the cross-beam hard against his abdomen. Rodrigo tells us only men work the loom because if women did it they would be unable to bear children. As the man yanks back on the beam it nearly lifts him off the dirt floor.

It begins to rain again. At the edge of another village in the middle of a corn field squats a mud and stick house with a red tiled roof. Outside, a batch of wool yarn soaks in a plastic bucket. The maroon dye is made from the shell of a palm nut, which grows in front of the house, mixed with ash and cooked. Inside the dark interior a man weaves tapestries on an upright loom. Candles tied to the loom drip wax over the wooden beams. The French toss candy to the kids, and we move on.

Near the road we enter another house. Three ancient foosball tables with metal players grace the entrance. A man snores on a couch in front of a TV. We descend narrow stairs to a basement full of long, white strands of agave leaf that have been beaten with rocks. The man collects his drunken self from the couch, overlooking his pants zipper, to show us the process in which agave is made into the ubiquitous fifty pound sugar sacks.

First the strands are cleaned and smoothed by whacking a bunch of leaves against a platform of nails mounted on a pillar. Next it's put on a tall dowel, not unlike cotton candy, and taken into a dark room with a low ceiling. A claptrap contraption of metal wheels and fanbelts clanks into action with the flip of a switch. The agave strands are spun into thin twine. As the machine clatters loudly, the room fills with agave fibers. After five minutes it becomes hard to breathe. These machines are often worked by children. The twine is then put on looms and woven into a loose weave. The rolls of woven agave are then shipped off to be cut and sewn into sacks.

Not necessarily for sugar, these sacks are used to carry everything. Looping a strap around the load and across the head, a campesino carries a load of potatoes, wood, corn, clothes. I was even advised to get a sack for my backpack as protection against slashing and oil and grease from buses.

Our last stop is high in the hills to visit an old man who makes beautiful colored boxes. Many years ago, he married his niece to keep land in the family. With the parents themselves the products of inbreeding, four of their five children are severely retarded.

The 87-year-old man, who cannot speak, makes the boxes out of strips of mountain bamboo. He sits on a reed mat with the brightly colored strips spread before him: red, green, yellow, blue, orange. He rocks slowly back and forth holding the strips in his toothless mouth. Deftly using both hands and feet, he weaves them into boxes. Each box fits inside the next largest box until the smallest is no bigger than a thumbnail. This is all he has done for as long as anyone can remember. He learned to make boxes from his father who learned from his father. Now he is the only one left as his son does not want to learn and the other son is too mentally handicapped. The secret of the boxes will die.

Victor Von Hagen in *Ecuador the Unknown*, describes how the barter system once operated in Otavalo:

> A woman wishing to sell a pile of Indian peppers arranged them neatly before her. A prospective 'buyer,' or better— 'trader'—sat down opposite her with a large sack of maize kernels. Not a word was uttered. The buyer reached into her sack and extracted handful after handful of the maize. The one trading peppers fixed her eyes on the mounting pile; the one trading maize for peppers kept her eyes on the face of the other. When the trader saw the faintest shadow of satisfaction crossing the face of the other, she stopped piling the grain and the woman with the peppers would, if she deemed the return sufficient, reach out and draw in the maize while the other picked up her peppers. But there might be considerable wrangling; if the maize-trader believed the pepper woman too greedy, she would go elsewhere to begin the bargaining anew. Transactions necessarily took a great deal of time. At these *catus*, or markets, Inca law did not fix a standard of value, for this was left entirely to the satisfaction of the parties involved.

The U.S. market for handicrafts has enabled the Otavaleños to keep their culture and way of life somewhat intact. Throughout the Americas, the indigenous people are the poorest of the poor; here in Otavalo they are actually making a decent living. In fact, one even sees Otavaleños selling sweaters in New York, when for most Ecuadorians going to the United States is a far away dream. Yet the fashion demand for sweaters (Shit, I have two.), has created a caste system between Otavalo and the villages.

Late afternoon on market day ,an Otavaleño shops for an electric iron with his wife while their daughter waits in the Chevy Trooper. It's easy to point a finger at the Otavaleños, but looking closer all I see is a mirror. I wonder how much of <u>my</u> buying power comes at the expense of others.

A couple days later, Gerard and I decide to climb Imbabura, a 4,360 meter extinct volcano, to get in shape for Cotopaxi, while Philippe continues his tour of South America heading for Columbia. With not very explicit directions from Rodrigo, we step off a bus in a small village. The mountain rises straight before us.

"I think we should go back to town and get a truck to take us up the road," says Gerard.

"Oh, it can't be that far. Let's just walk."

Of course he's right, but we end up doing it the hard way. We self-consciously puff and haul our packs past the fincas and campesinos staring at us. They must think us complete idiots. Imbabura occasionally comes out of the clouds teasing us. The view is beautiful in the evening light.

A boy runs by us.

"NO!" he yells shaking his head. *"No es possible."*

Now what does that mean? Is it physically not possible to climb the mountain? Or do they not want us here? Is it not possible to cross this land? Plagued by doubts and fatigue, we slow our pace. It looks like we're on the wrong ridge. I insist we can cross over and gain the next ridge. Gerard points out there's a cliff in the way. Soon, it becomes obvious we won't be climbing Imbabura taking this approach.

It's growing dark, and we're uncomfortable with camping in someone's finca, so we decide to descend. About halfway down we are accosted by three very drunk men. One of them informs us that this is his land were crossing.

"We're just walking down to the road," I say.

"You can't cross this land."

"Okay. We'll just head over and down the road."

"You have to pay us to cross this land."

They begin getting a little too close. Two of them have isolated Gerard and are hassling him, grabbing his arm demanding payment.

"We don't have any money," I lie.

"You have to pay us."

Things are getting tense and happening a little too fast.

"Give us some food," they demand.

This could be an easy out.

"Well, let's see what we've got," I say and drop my pack.

Lying on top is a box of Oreos.

"Here, how 'bout some cookies?"

"Compadre."

"Amigo."

Suddenly we've got three drunken buddies. We quickly depart while their faces are full.

"Dude, that could have been serious trouble. I was looking for a knife. You should never take off your pack. I saw that and thought it was all over," Gerard says.

"I had to get the cookies."

"Yeah, but they could've knifed you right there. I was ready to break that fucker's arm."

Gerard's from New York. He knows how to deal with people.

The bus driver charges us double to return to Quito because we put our packs on the seats of the empty bus instead of on top. Too haggard to argue, we pay him.

I need to connect all of this: Robbery, feeling degraded, poverty, exploitation, TV sets and no running water, organ theft, fear of being in a foreign country, fear of being foreign. There's something going on here, a desperation, an agitated anxious air like before a thunderstorm when horses prance about nervous and excited. The world has been turned on edge. I'm walking a thin, dark line. I feel values shifting under me like solid ground turning liquid during an earthquake. I can no longer be <u>sure</u> of anything.

Quito—
City of Atahualpa

Suddenly, you realize that simply by accepting so many of the things that you take for granted, or simply by not protesting against things you feel may be wrong, or simply by refusing to educate yourself to the consequences of your own life and your own actions and the actions of your society upon other human beings and the planet at large, you are choosing to march through the 20th Century as a kind of insane, psychopathic murderer, a participant in the planned destruction of the planet. —John Nichols

Upon returning to Quito, the possibility of climbing Cotopaxi pushes my anxieties and questions to a deep hollow at the base of my consciousness. At the Gran Casino, Gerard and I hook up with a Canadian couple, Cody and Dana, who is five months pregnant. Delayed by a stolen VISA card and traveler's checks and a lack of climbing partners Cody has been waiting to climb for three weeks and is getting anxious.

Cody works for PetroCanada and somehow during our acquaintance we avoid discussion of the petroleum development in the rainforest, restricting our conversation to climbing.

After receiving repeated warnings that it is the most dangerous place in the city, Cody urges us to hike up the Panicillo, the hill overlooking Quito, from the Gran Casino. Gerard mentions the reports of armed robbery, rape, tourists getting cameras ripped off. One taxi driver said someone ran up to his taxi and seized the sunglasses off his face. But at six in the morning all seems calm, the abandoned streets and morning air evaporates my fears, although I keep a watchful eye as we ascend the narrow stairways. Just in case.

At the crest of the Panicillo rises a monstrous concrete statute of La Virgin with wings and halo. She delicately holds a chain leading to the collar of a hideous lizard-like creature withering beneath her feet.

Walking around the Virgin and looking north we can see the mountains near Otavalo where we previously camped. The extinct volcanos of Imbabura and Cayambe, Ecuador's third highest peak, tower above the paramo. And to the south squats the perfect snow covered cone of Cotopaxi. Below spreads Quito; the spires of the Cathedral poke above the grey fog of diesel.

Above the city jut the green slopes of Pichincha as if trying to distance itself from the urban sprawl spiraling up the mountain. Although quiet now, over the past centuries Pichincha occasionally erupted destroying Quito, which was subsequently rebuilt each time. In 1822 on the slopes of Pichincha, General Jose de Sucre and the forces of Simon Bolivar defeated the Spanish, liberating Ecuador. Bolivar envisioned a great republic of Venezuela, Columbia and Ecuador. But massive political bickering prevented the Republic of Gran Columbia, and in 1830 Ecuador broke away.

Gerard and I had wanted to climb Pichincha but were dissuaded by the accounts of violence. Apparently a crazed man with a gun lives in a cave there and is known to rob and rape unwary gringos. Cody and Dana, however, climbed the 15,400 peak a few days ago without any problems and act incredulous that we'd let something like that stop us.

As we descend the steep steps of the Panicillo back into Quito, the city erupts in full throbbing frenzy. Women wash clothes at the communal water trough. Prisoners howl at us behind prison bars. A huge rat gnaws at the carcass of a small dog half buried in ancient refuse.

Padlocked metal doors clatter open, revealing rows of shoes, batteries, candy, bread, fruit, whole chickens roasting on a spit, gum, Fruit (the orange and red soft drinks), stereos, watches, sunglasses. (You never see anyone actually wearing sunglasses, yet they are sold on every corner.) *Todo es negociable.* Everything is negotiable.

Many families live above or next to their stalls. Some stalls are merely the doorway, the door swung wide. Some doorways open like a closet full of dirt and post war rubble. Men shovel the dirt out. This puzzles me until we walk by a hillside lined with houses and I see they are excavating the slopes for more living space. A tiny brick building sits surrounded by hill until somebody builds a wall and starts hauling the earth away.

Girls in school uniforms perch on park benches in the plaza, their shoes shined by boys dressed in rags. An old Indian woman sleeps in a famous cathedral doorway, a fine example of Spanish colonial architecture says the guide book. Rickety bamboo scaffolds spiderweb up the grey, imposing edifice.

Across from the cathedral, men rip up concrete with picks and sledge hammers. At night, floodlights illuminate the street while they work.

"It's a good thing they don't have jackhammers or it would be ungodly noisy," says Gerard.

The picks and hammers mix with the traffic noises bouncing off the slate colonial buildings on either side of the narrow street choked with cars with bad rings and buses spewing diesel exhaust. The streets clog, the cars and buses stop for a short period, then everything surges forward in a short, jerky motion like corpuscles in the bloodstream. It's faster to walk, dodging the throng of people weaving in and out of the traffic.

"It's just like a movie," teases Gerard and we laugh.

There are virtually no stoplights, and stop signs are rare. I doubt if there are any traffic laws. Cars, trucks loaded with bananas, taxis, people, all move through the streets with little regard for life or limb. Yet seemingly no one gets killed. I have yet to see a death or even an accident. Later I discover that you go to jail for getting in an accident, and there is no car insurance. Cars are outrageously expensive. New cars cost at least three times what they do in the States; even a beat-up Toyota sells for $3000. So people are actually very careful. It just seems chaotic.

As we round the corner to mail a few postcards, the market maelstrom descends upon us. We need to keep moving and keep our eyes in front of us or else run the danger of being run down by an orange truck with no brakes or a *campesino* bent double carting a side of meat or fifty pound sack of sugar. I steal a quick glance at the small yellow potatoes, the red potatoes, the purple potatoes, the stacks of yuca, the orange potatoes, tomatoes, chilies, multi-hued potatoes, baskets of dried herbs, peppers, rice, chicken carcasses, heaps of red, purple and yellow, and black corn, the baby lying in a cardboard box, the mother smoking a cigarette and breathing exhaust fumes. At least I can always spot Gerard towering above the crowd in his white hat with the red light flashing "tourist," "tourist".

Come evening, a family beds down in front of the bank. Nearby in the shadows a man in a suit presses against a woman in a blue dress. The smell of calcified urine haunts every corner.

The next day we walk to New Town past the U.S. Embassy fortress, past the graffiti praising Sadam Hussein and condemning the United States. Philip Agee, in *Inside the Company* points out that graffiti is often CIA sponsored; local protesters are too poor to afford spray paint. He writes that it's typical for the CIA to sponsor anti-U.S. propaganda to convince local governments they need CIA support, not unlike an insurance sales-men setting a small fire.

In the business district downtown, men in suits carrying leather brief-cases stroll by the gringo sidewalk cafes and tourist shops. Each bank sports a least one guard with a sawed off shotgun. Quichua women in shawls peddle jewelry, sweaters, candy, lottery tickets, weavings, gum. There are stop signs and stop lights in New Town, large hotels, stores, hookers, and the cab drivers wear ties. In New Town there are clean sidewalks.

Embassy staffs and oil executives live in New Town in houses with gardens—flowers, lilies, orchids, and trees lined safely behind walls topped with broken glass. Ford Broncos, Toyota trucks and BMW's sit parked behind locked portals. Dobermans growl from the roof tops. An armed guard is stationed in a mobile guard house at every corner. Some houses have their own guards.

Poverty, overpopulation, exploitation, greed, inequitable distribution of land—revolution seems eminent. Except that everyone is too busy try-ing to make a living to think about revolution. Revolutions take time. Revolution means starving and sprawling though the mud worrying about getting shot.

Boys—seven and eight years old, some fifteen, some young as four, pester us for shoe shines. I raise my ratty tennis shoes; they insist on clean-ing them. I think about giving the beggars and shoeshine boys a few sucres but the guide books say giving creates dependence.

I feel uncomfortable with all this begging, not that panhandling is new to me, I've never felt comfortable with it. I never know how much to give. Is twenty sucres an insult? Is that just a rationalization? I invent all sorts of excuses for bypassing the beggar, but they all ring hollow.

Kaes says that in India parents purposefully mutilate their younger chil-dren so they can make money begging. Begging is not only accepted but encouraged outside the temples. People always give money to the beggars as a sort of Karmic insurance policy.

On the Quito streets you can walk right past and shake your head and not look beggars in the eye. But sitting at the cafe they come up to your table when you're trying to relax on vacation enjoying a Pilsner and hold out their hand and wait. Ignoring them does no good; they aren't in any hurry. And as soon as you drop a few sucres into their hand, you're surrounded. Nobody hassles you for money in Old Town. They glance at the gringos who must be lost and hurry on their way.

A week later I found myself standing outside a shabby hotel in a small village getting some fresh air. A heavy fog hung in the night air, pierced only by the town's single street light. On a board with wheels, a boy crippled by polio and wearing a cardboard sign around his neck singled me out, pushed himself up to me and held out his hand. I looked to friends on either side for some signal. After an awkward pause in which it was obvious I couldn't ignore him, I dropped a wad of crumbled bills into his hand. He nodded and wheeled himself over to the arriving bus and flopped up the steps of the bus to beg.

Gerard and I see a place advertised as a quiet English pub. Thinking a change from Pilsner would be nice, visions of Guinness dancing in our heads, we check it out. The door is locked. (Who ever heard of a locked bar? This should have been our first clew.) Ringing a buzzer brings a napper fellow who greets us in English, and bids us enter. Already I feel uneasy. Several well-dressed men and women sit in large comfortable chairs speaking English in low voices. The bartender may be Ecuadorian. I have to concentrate to ask for a beer in my native tongue. They have two kinds, Club and Pilsner, no different except the cost, three dollars each. No Guinness, no porter, no darts.

Not only is the beer six times as expensive, this place denies that it is even in Ecuador. As much as I wanted a refuge from the city, stepping into the plush green and mahogany room is like stepping aboard a spaceship. You can't even see out the windows. You are isolated. Removed. As Gerard says, "Denial ain't no river in Egypt." I feel less uncomfortable in a corner bar with flies and cracked vinyl booths. The bathrooms here are very nice, though. Is this what we've done with our affluence in America: bought insulation from the rest of the world? We pad our lives with dollars instead of fiberglass, but things continue to leak in around the edges.

The Inca historian, Garcilaso de la Vega (1539-1616) wrote that Quito was ruled by "a powerful lord, as cruel as he was crude and belligerent, and, consequently, dreaded by all his neighbors." For the Inca conquest of Quito, "Tupac Inca recruited forty thousand fighting men." He tells us the siege lasted three to five years under command of Prince Huayna Capac. "King Quito died of grief when he saw that practically all of his land had been conquered," wrote Garcilaso.

Inca Huayna Capac established Quito as the northern capital of his empire, the largest on earth, as a sailor from Genoa "discovered" and subsequently named, the West Indies. Thirty years later, Huayna Capac was informed of bearded white men in ships exploring the coast of his northern domain. When Francisco Pizzaro returned to Panama for more ships and men to continue his explorations, he left two men behind on Gallo Isle, off the coast of present day Ecuador. These two men, who have long faded into history, more than any other factor, precipitated the downfall of the Inca Empire.

Huayna Capac ordered the two men, one white, one black, to be brought before him. Whether or not they arrived in Quito or were killed by the coastal inhabitants is unknown. However legend has it that Huayna Capac received a vision of half a million ghosts arrayed to attack shortly before his death from smallpox in 1527. According to Pedro de Cieza de León, the chronicler of the Spanish conquest, the massive smallpox epidemic killed over 200,000 people.

Upon his death, Huayna Capac divided the empire between his two sons, Huascar of Cuzco and his favorite son, Atahualpa, born of the union of Huayna and Paccha, the Cara princess of the newly acquired territory north of Quito. Atahualpa assumed control of the northern empire, with Quito as the capital. Civil war soon broke out between the half brothers with Atahualpa controlling the army, while the Inca citizenry remained loyal to Huascar. Not surprisingly Atahualpa emerged victorious. Other than his deceased father, Atahualpa had no link to the royal family or Inca system. Removed from Inca sovereignty, Atahualpa freely killed royalty and devastated regions loyal to Huascar. He was regarded as a savage outsider. As Atahualpa marched south with over one hundred thousand troops to assume control of Cuzco, the Inca capital, Francisco Pizzaro and 150 Spanish conquistadors had landed near present day Guayaquil and were picking their way down the coast.

Preoccupied with victory, Atahualpa did not concern himself with the small band of foreigners. At their first meeting, in Cajamarca in northern Peru, Pizzaro captured Atahualpa in a surprise attack, and his men slaughtered thousands of confused and unarmed Indians. Atahualpa promised the Spanish a room full of gold in exchange for his freedom. The Spanish held him prisoner for several months while some eleven tons of gold objects poured in from all corners of the empire. Pre-Inca temples, as well as Cuzco, were raided. When the room was filled, Pizzaro ordered the strangulation of Atahualpa and the meltdown of the gold.

Had Pizzaro attempted his invasion when he first sailed down the coast a few years earlier, it's extremely doubtful he would have succeeded against a unified Inca Empire. Only because of the smallpox epidemic and subsequent civil war and dissatisfaction with Atahualpa was a small invasion force able to conquer the most extensive empire in the new world. After the execution of Atahualpa, Pizzaro marched on to the capital portraying himself as the liberator of Cuzco from the army of the usurper Atahualpa.

Completing their conquest of the disarrayed Inca empire, the Spanish turned their attention north to Quito, which they reasoned must be as rich in gold as Cuzco. Ruminavi, Atahualpa's last remaining captain, still commanded a large army in Quito. Unlike Atahualpa's army in Peru, this was not an army of occupation, but one loyal to Atahualpa and ready to revenge his death and fight for their homeland against the invading Spanish. With thousands of troops, Ruminavi repeatedly battled the Spanish on their march across the paramo. However thousands of Indians proved little match for a few hundred Spanish armed with steel and horses.

By the time they reached Quito four months later, Ruminavi had razed the city, and ashes and stone were all that was left for the Spanish. The Spanish tortured the surrendered captains to get them to reveal the location of Atahualpa's hidden treasure, of which they knew nothing. Rumors of this gold treasure persisted, leading Gonzalo Pizzaro on his ill-fated journey. If they ever existed, the treasures of Quito have never been recovered, and still lure the occasional treasure hunter to the moist forests beyond the eastern cordillera.

Containing 900,000 people, Quito is the second highest capital in the world, after La Paz, Bolivia. (If one does not count Llasa, Tibet, presently occupied by the Chinese.) At 9300 feet I get sunburned walking through the park on my way to the archeology museum buried on the fifth floor of the Central Bank.

In the manner that North American anthropologists insist upon the Bering Strait migration, numerous diagrams and references in the museum indicate that Polynesian island-hopping, raft-riding explorers colonized South America, offering an intriguing commentary on North-South perspectives.

Ecuador's cultural diversity is as varied as its topography. However, all that has been recovered, from scores of cultures dating between 3000 B.C. and 1500 A.D., are a few ceramic figures. No text accompanies the figures. Stone figurines and pottery litter the coastal areas, and are picked up and sold on the streets of Quito or plowed under. Occasionally gold fishhooks and rings are found and sold or hoarded.

The museum classifies indigenous cultures in a strange manner: the structure of their skulls indicating what kind of "human species" they are. One culture strapped boards to the front and back of their children's heads. After three years, the skull retained a long pointed shape. The Incas called these people Palta, or avocado, describing the shape of their heads.

Civilizations in the Ecuadorian Andes once rivaled the Incas themselves, with the first evidence of worked platinum, and perhaps the world's finest goldsmiths. Their work, small gold pieces, rings, earrings, and cups line the walls of the gold room displaying pieces spared from the Spanish ransom of Atahualpa.

Testifying to the skill of these ancient artisans, the mask of the sun, glowing with it's own luminescence, scowls from the center of the wall. Hammered from gold, two snarling jaguars perch on a condor's head, forming the face of the mask. Dozens of paper thin gold snakes intertwine as hair; a head or hand protrudes from the beak of the condor. The mask depicts the holy trinity of Jaguar, Condor, and Serpent, representing power, vision and wisdom. The mythological importance of the jaguar and serpent gives rise to speculation that the mighty civilizations of the Andes trace their roots back to the jungle cultures which still hold the jaguar and snake in everyday fear and awe.

I must spend an inordinate time staring at the mask, for a woman in a red dress approaches and begins talking to me about the Incas. I'm suspicious of why a pretty, well dressed woman would suddenly begin talking to me, until I realize I must be a curiosity. Doctura Moryma Veronica Vinocuna Ureña, a dentist on her day off, offers to show me the colonial art museum on the sixth floor of the Central Bank.

The colonial art museum consists of a row of Virgin paintings and a room of bloody Jesuses. I've never seen so many Virgins in my life. Veronica asks me what religion I am and seems a little taken aback when I say "none." I don't even try to explain Black Pantheism or Coyote Cult. I manage to point out the irony of all the cherubs and apostles in the paintings having blue eyes. Veronica isn't fazed by my cynicism saying, "*Claro*, Catholicism came from Europe, and we've accepted it."

Leaving the museum, we take an afternoon beer across the street. Veronica asks how I find Ecuador. When I mention my frustration over *precio gringo*, she patiently illustrates the concept of *se depende* to me. If you look like you can afford it, you get charged a higher price. Those who look destitute pay less. At first this strikes me as grossly unfair. Why should I be charged twice that of someone else?

Then I realize that *se depende* is a method of distributing wealth, sort of a popular tax system. The merchants aren't getting rich. Besides, so what if I get gypped out of twenty cents here and fifty cents there? It's a gringo tax. How many Ecuadorians feel justified in soaking a gringo? Have we not been fleecing the rest of the world for years?

No matter how little money I may actually have, I will never truly know poverty. The real difference between rich and poor is that we can make <u>choices</u> which affect our lives.

Ecuadorians bemoan the high cost of books and computers. Paperbacks range from $15-$20 and personal computers cost well over three times as much as in the States. When I express surprise that books and computers are taxed while gasoline and pharmaceuticals are subsidized, Veronica explains that the government is not interested in furthering education but in lining their pockets.

"One bunch of crooks gets in power and gets everything they can before another bunch comes along and throws them out so they can have a chance to get rich," she says.

Veronica makes artificial Bonsai trees from corn flower paste. She shows me her kit, a leaf for a model, wires for stems, metal cookie cutters to cut out the leaves, several tubes of oil paints to paint the cutout leaves. It takes years to cultivate real Bonsai trees, she tells me.

Obscured by Clouds

The man who doesn't like clouds
Has no business coming to Ecuador.
They're the faithful dogs of the mountain,
Huge, faithful dogs;
Loftily crowning the horizon;
The place's altitude is some ten thousand feet,
                    so they say,
It's hard, they say, on your heart, stomach, and
                    breathing,
And on every inch of the foreigner's body.
—Henri Michaux, 1928.

Around a wobbly wooden table at the Gran Casino dining room, we form an international climbing party for our assault on Cotopaxi. Cody, from Canada, is the acknowledged leader as he is the only one with any real experience. Joining us will be Oscar, a jolly, bearded business man from Chile. I'm not sure what exactly he does, but he's the only person who leaves the Gran Casino every morning wearing a suit, after gulping down several cups of coffee. He nods his head excitedly before dashing out when Cody reaffirms our climbing plans for Saturday. Gerard opts to sit this climb out. I think he feels apprehensive about our lack of experience. Ralph, from Germany, who Cody met a couple days previously, fills in. Ralph is reserved, but seems self-assured. Like a pickup game of basketball, we quickly introduce ourselves, sizing each other up and hoping for the best. At the last minute, Kaes and Marti decide to tag along with Gerard and Dana for a view of the mountain and to offer moral support.

It turns into an all day hassle just getting to the climbing refuge at the base of Cotopaxi's cone. The bus to the nearby town of Latacunga takes an extra hour because of a collision between a gas truck and another bus on the highway. By the time we pass by, the fire is out and the blackened hull of the bus sits empty, precariously perched over the ravine.

The Latacunga Saturday market appears chaotic. All the caminoetta (small pickup truck) drivers say the road is very bad, and they can't make it. We finally find a man with a Toyota pickup who will take us for thirty dollars, a bit steep. Before leaving town he has to get a park license which takes another half hour. It begins to rain so he stops by his house to rig a tarp over the bed of the truck where four of us must ride. We can either stand in the pouring rain or huddle under the tarp inhaling exhaust leaking up through the truck bed.

As we pull up to the entrance of Cotopaxi National Park, a climbing party of young Ecuadorians sits huddled in the rain hoping for a ride. The oldest and group leader can't be more than sixteen. I met him yesterday in Quito while renting climbing gear. He said this was his second time up Cotopaxi; he'd already climbed all the peaks around Quito. They asked us for a ride up to the *refugio*. I immediately offer room in the truck, however our driver steadfastly refuses any more passengers.

I begin to understand why as we ascend the dirt road across the paramo. His truck is possibly the world's slowest vehicle. It takes three hours just to get to the refugio. While the road is indeed rough, it's nothing formidable. The truck, though, is not up to the task. Bad compression and a loose clutch are more to blame than the road.

It takes constant coaxing from Marti sitting in front bargaining continually for each bend in the road, her "You won't be paid" countering his "The truck can't make it." We have to push the truck up the steep part of the road and walk to lighten the load.

Rounding a bend we see the driver unloading. He refuses to go any farther. The refugio is visible above us at the base of the glacier covered cone. It doesn't look too far, but at 4800 meters (15,360 feet) it takes over an hour of heavy breathing to walk up to the large cabin. Cody, Oscar and I make two trips to get all the gear and food. It's five o'clock by the time we finally get settled in and everyone is thoroughly exhausted by the day's frustration and altitude.

At sundown the rain finally stops, and the sky clears. A beautiful sunset promises a clear day tomorrow. The clouds stretch below us in all directions like being in an airplane. The volcanic cones of Cayambe, sixty-five miles away, and Cotopaxi, the only landscape this side of the clouds, glow from below by the setting sun.

Cotopaxi towers above us, hurling down tongues of ice. A black wall of rock is visible just below the summit, the *Llanastacha*, "black rock" in Quichua. Cotopaxi has often been compared to paintings of Mount Fujiyama, which seems a great injustice to both peaks.

It is not the rendering of nature into art that disturbs me so much as comparisons in which the art predominates over nature as if art itself contained the beauty rather than represented it. Cotopaxi, or any mountain for that matter is far more sublime than any human created art. The eons of sculpting a mountain exceed not only human lifetimes but even our existence as a species. I have yet to see a human create a mountain. I don't mean a trash heap or rounded ski hill, but a rocky peak scoured by glaciers into quebradas, arêtes, couloirs, hanging valleys, and false summits. We can't do it. In our celebration of landscape art are we not attempting to encapsulate and contain nature's power?

In 1877 Cotopaxi erupted sending a column of ash twice the height of the mountain, turning the sky to night at eight a.m. in Quito. This eruption melted the glacier causing massive flooding all the way to Esmaraldes on the coast 150 miles away. I admit I have some apprehension about climbing a live volcano.

We put on a big pot of water to make spaghetti, and two hours later we're eating the worst meal any of us have ever had. Water boils at a very low temperature at 15,000 feet, and it takes forever to cook. The spaghetti is inedible.

During the evening the young Ecuadorians, boys really, arrive after hitching a couple rides and walking a good part of the way. They're in bed by the time we finish picking at our dinner. Cody is relieved to find that one of the other parties has a professional guide. We will discreetly tag behind since none of us know the route. Too excited to sleep, the guided party plays with their clanking gear all hours. And the refugio caretaker has invited some friends up for beers and a Friday night poker game. Noise and a growling stomach keep me awake all night.

We arise at one a.m. and wait for the guided group to leave so we can follow them. I'm too groggy to realize fully how unprepared they are. We are finally underway at 2:30. Not taking any chances with La Tourista, I chase a Lomatil with Pepto Bismol.

We forge a slow trudge through the mud and scree to the base of the glacier. *I can't do this*, flashes through my mind. A cold wind chills us as we struggle to put on our crampons in the dark and rope up. In the past few hours the weather turned partly cloudy and very windy. The summit is cloaked by clouds.

We follow the guided party of five onto the glacier. I'm the last one. With everyone roped together and surrounded by snow, it looks like an Antarctic expedition.

In the dim light of an obscured half moon, the headlamps of another climbing party bob across the ice field descending toward us. The steep slope and blowing snow conspire with the altitude making travel extremely slow. The returning party of the four young Ecuadorians reports bad weather forced them to abandon the climb.

The guided party begins having problems. They walk a few dozen meters at a time and flop down on the snow to rest. We soon forgo our plan of following and instead pass them. Now I see why they are having so much trouble. Most are dressed in jeans, one guy doesn't even have gloves. They must be freezing. I'm decked out in full winter regalia, several layers of polypro, wool sweater, pile, Gore-Tex, and I still feel a chill. Later we find out their guide was some local climber who met the clients in the super posh Hotel Oro Verde and said he'd take them up for $100 each.

In the poor visibility and flat light, Oscar nearly falls into a crevasse before Cody yanks him back. We cross the crevasse on a narrow ice bridge. Holes in the ice drop away into nothingness. One step off the bridge and you would plummet, which is why we're roped together. If one falls, the others dig their ice axes in and prevent him from dropping more than a few feet. Last night, Cody explained how we would get someone back out but I'm not sure I really understood it. Something to do with triangulation.

The crevasse stretches out into the dim predawn light huge and terrifyingly beautiful. It opens up five meters and drops out of sight, yawning like a great baleen whale. Icicles droop down the opposite face. I have this urge to plunge into the void and be swallowed like an icy Jonah.

At dawn the sky lightens gradually; however, nothing appears distinct as we are in the middle of a cloud. Another climbing party turns back; the weather worsens and the glacier steepens. The weather looks grim, and we don't know the route. So naturally we continue.

A few minutes later the sun breaks through the clouds making everything worthwhile. The universe spreads out beneath us, opening up, in one of those lifetime moments when you sense you are being allowed too much. The possibility of the infinite. A thick bank of clouds insulates us from the world like a floor of milk. Removed, we watch the planet spin below. Once we witness the world from another perspective we can never return to innocence or pretend ignorance. Centrifugal force pushes me to the edge, but not without the corresponding emotional and epistemological vertigo. It is at the edges we discover the center.

Nothing exists save the clouds below, the great glacier, the blue sky surrounding us and the sun frying our skulls and faces. Huge crevasses flow frozen down the mountain of ice. The volcanic cone rises above us another thousand feet. The other climbers are now dots picking their way down. Heartened by the sun, the beauty and visibility we march on. It's seven a.m.

I hear a shout and look up. Oscar is waving his arms. His sunglasses tumble by me just out of reach. They pick up speed on the slope, then slow. It looks like they may stop, but they continue rolling over the edge and into a crevasse.

Every time we stop for a break, the altitude demands all my mental energy to secure my pack to my ice axe plunged to the hilt in the snow to prevent a similar fate for my pack. The altitude makes everything an ordeal. Strapping the pack to the axe, taking out a water bottle, unscrewing the lid, holding the bottle and lid without dropping it takes utmost concentration. It's like being underwater; everything occurs in slow motion. I have barely broken a sweat, yet I have to stop every ten meters to catch my breath. My legs are fine, but I can scarcely put one foot in front of the other. My head pounds, pounds, pounds like an Excederin commercial waiting for the soothing announcer. *Drink more water,* I tell myself. But I don't feel thirsty. I can't feel the water as I pour it down my throat. I plod along, dizzy and nauseous, on autopilot aware only of my pounding head. I vaguely perceive my body under me. But I can't feel it; it doesn't hurt. I'm unsure that it's even mine.

At 18,000 feet, we take a break, and Oscar wanders off. Purple toilet paper goes whizzing by in the strong wind.

The weather turns worse, and clouds roll back in. The wind blows so hard we can't hear each other even when shouting at the top of our lungs. The black wall of *Llanastacha* appears like an apparition behind a curtain of clouds. Cody looks back and holds up his arms, questioning. "Forward," I signal. We are only an hour from the summit. Clouds and wind and snow obscure *Llanastacha* once more. Cody signals retreat at 5700 meters (18,700 feet). No one argues. Escape from worldly concerns appears impossible. The bonds of gravity are too great.

My head is about to erupt. I lead the way down stumbling and slipping. I can barely stand up much less see straight. The world spins. I act and move like I'm stone drunk. My head feels like the worst hangover I've ever had, but there's no fog inside my brain. Everything is sharp and clear, yet I can barely function. I collapse on the snow.

"Cody!" I yell, "Someone else better lead."

I plunge my axe into the snow and clip on to it, while I untie from the rope so I don't slide down the mountain.

We stumble down through the clouds. Oscar keeps falling. I feel like barfing. We stop to remove our crampons. I fall asleep sitting on the glacier.

The Indians of the Sierra believe they are descended from the volcanos Chimbarazo and Cotopaxi, and the spirits of dead shamans return to the volcanos. The curanderos or healers invoke these spirits of Cotopaxi for assistance in healing. In climbing mountains are we attempting to do the same? But what is our disease?

"Because it's there" seems a rather glib response to a perplexing question. It may not necessarily be the action, but the approach that is vital. If we climb to conquer, is this not emblematic of our domination over nature and thus a form of machismo?

If we climb to escape, we will be forced to return. It is this escape aspect which troubles me, perhaps because I find myself so engrossed with my needs for escape through outdoor recreation that I dismiss other concerns as secondary.

It may be that mountains contain something crucial missing from our lives. Mountains can teach us things, especially those of us too stubborn or arrogant to listen to other people and insist on doing everything the hard way. Some of us need to gaze into a crevasse in order to look into our own soul.

If we climb to learn, to gain perspective, to see, we may take that acquired knowledge back to the valleys. What can we learn from mountains? Knowledge and respect of creation and a familiarity with extremes which precludes parochialism.

Climbing mountains may just be an excuse to our goal oriented minds, much like hunting and fishing. The real goal is to be. To be outside, listening and learning. But all too often the clanking of carabiners drowns out the subtle voice of our real purpose.

PARADISE
BY THE SACRED WATERS

Don't come near, anyone,
Stand aside or go.
My disease is contagious,
I'm full of woe.

I'm alone, born alone,
Of a mother forlorn,
All alone I stay,
A feather in a storm.

Why should a painted house
Make a blind man sing?
What are balconies to the street,
If he can't see a thing?
—Ecuadorian poet, Juan León Mera

No longer bound together by the mountain, our climbing party quickly disintegrates on the highway in Latacunga. In a simultaneous decision, Cody, Dana, Oscar and Ralph head back to the Gran Casino. The rest of us search for a room in Latacunga. The first two hotels listed in the guide book are nonexistent. We finally find a rundown pension with dark green peeling paint and two bathrooms, but each room opens onto an open air courtyard with lots of flowers. *Not bad,* I think, but there are rumblings from Kaes and Marti. Their chronic dissatisfaction is becoming contagious. About nine o'clock we go looking for a place to eat dinner. The only thing open is a very greasy fried chicken joint. Kaes and Marti are in good humored dismay alternately griping and laughing over the place. Marti walks down the street to look for another restaurant. By now my expectations of Ecuadorian food are so low that I order a couple pieces of chicken and a double order of *papas fritas*, French fries, the gringo stable.

I always enjoyed the food on my travels through Mexico. I like beans and rice and tortillas and fish tacos. Unfortunately, like all generalities about Latin America, the idea that the food in one country is similar to another decomposes rapidly when confronted with a heaping plate of white rice and a tough, greasy drumstick. All over Ecuador the food varies little, this monotony surpassed only by the blandness of the meal itself. The main fare consists of rice and chicken, or rice and beef supplanted with a hunk of boiled yuca, or manioc, perhaps the starchiest substance in existence.

Because of cholera the seafood is *verboten*, although many times I'm tempted to give ceviche a try. It amazes me that in a land with so much abundance the food is so dreary.

The following day Gerard takes lodging at Kaes and Marti's hotel in Quito. It becomes painfully obvious Gerard and I have different objectives. He tells me he wants to stay in Quito, take Spanish lessons and live with a family for four weeks. I can't bear spending four weeks in Quito. I'm not a city person. There's more mountains to climb, and I still want to check out Peru and Bolivia, but to be on my own like Philippe frightens me.

I hate thinking of a friendship dissolving like this. I guess I thought we were compatible—had the same interests and values, but maybe I was just projecting my interests assuming they were his. If I had paid more attention earlier, I would have seen this coming and understood it better. Perhaps.

Relaxing in a sunny courtyard, Grateful Dead oozing from the stereo, La Casona, sort of a guest house, run by Mario, an Argentinian craftsman and his sculptor girlfriend, makes a nice refuge from the city. There's even a guest kitchen, and I quickly load up at the market on fresh fruits and vegetables. Summer begins, and suddenly there's a lot of gringos running around downtown.

Returning the climbing gear, I realize that an ice axe is the ultimate urban defence weapon. I've never felt safer. No one is going to mess with this nasty looking thing. It's light, feels good in your hands, has all sorts of uses, like prying your way onto a crowded bus.

Crossing a busy street at the same moment, I encounter Britta Hanson, her long blond hair hard to miss here. We begin an instant conversation, agree to meet later for coffee which turns into dinner. Britta, a healthy Wisconsin girl, studying in Quito on a Fulbright scholarship, is one of those vivacious and captivating personalities.

"On a beach in Brazil without a dime we ate coconuts," she says pulling her hair behind her ears.

"I was so hungry. It was great," she laughs.

"In the jungle, I lived with this Brazilian family. Everyone in the village had to come see the American. They taught me how to wash clothes. 'See the American, we have to teach her how to wash clothes,' they told everyone. They did everything with such care and precision. I would wash a dish and they would rewash it, polishing every inch." She rubs the whisky glass rim. "It was so sensual, like meditation."

"They were so happy, always laughing. We slept on the floor. Sometimes when we woke up, there wasn't enough food for breakfast, but it was okay. I slept with the kids. I got scabies. 'If you lie with the dogs, you're going to get fleas,' my father always said. But who wants to live life tepid?"

Britta suggests I make my way south and over to the coast to a place called Alandaluz. She also mentions a butterfly ranch near Coca. While I try to imagine a butterfly saddle and a butterfly roundup, she explains that a Peace Corps worker is helping people raise butterflies as a cash crop. Apparently, there is a big market for butterflies among collectors. I guess I can add butterflies to my list of collections. I'm beginning to feel like I need to make a transition, from collecting to participating.

Oxygen deprivation at high altitude must cause brain damage in climbers. Cody wants to attempt Chimborazo, the highest mountain in Ecuador, next week. I'm feeling claustrophobic in Quito and it seems that *soroche,* or altitude sickness, the pollution of Quito, and traveler's stress has triggered a chronic lung infection, (a previous condition from a combination of childhood asthma and fighting forest fires) so I retreat to the hot baths in the small town of Baños to recover.

In Baños, "The Telluride of Ecuador," all the hotels rent climbing gear, and bananas and sugarcane grow in the canyons and on the hillsides. As you step off the bus you're greeted by rows of stalls selling sugarcane and *jugo de caña.* Walking down the main street you see taffy being pulled at every other shop. On small sidewalk grills, *cuy,* or guinea pig, the delicacy of the Andes, lie roasting naked and spreadeagled, their ferocious jaws pried open and lips peeled back over their teeth. Normally adventurous when it comes to trying new food, I can't quite convince myself to eat one.

Heated by the thermal waters rising from the volcano Tungurahua, the "Our Lady of the Sacred Water Municipal Swimming Pool and Hot Springs" sits at the base of a hundred foot waterfall. The waterfall flows into a concrete aqueduct with periodic spouts where women slap clothes clean. I have a long talk in the baths with an Ecuadorian school teacher. Funny how most conversations sooner or later turn to Ecuador's *problems*. He says most of the country's troubles are alcoholism, lack of education and no one willing to work for change.

The town church is dedicated to La Virgin de Agua Santa. In front of the church you can buy Virgin paintings, Virgin key chains, Virgin medallions, Virgin earrings. Even my room key has a decal of La Virgin on it.

Off to the side of the nave, a wide hall leads to the small chapel of the Virgin. Numerous plaques of thanks and scribbled letters on the crumbling yellow walls attest to the Virgin's benevolence, while murals along the wall depict her miracles. The largest scene, nearly ten feet long, shows how in a fire a man placed the Virgin outside his building, and it was spared. Several leg braces, casts, and slings hang along the foyer, testimony to their owners' recovery after praying to the Virgin. I finally reach the large wooden Virgin and have to suppress laughter, as the priest is standing there. She looks nothing like the pictures I'm used to seeing of the Virgin Mary, but more like a cartoon caricature. She wears a blank expression like one of those dopey dolls you might win at a cheap amusement park. It seems each town in Ecuador has its own Virgin and they all look different, but why did Baños pick the Howdy-Doody Virgin?

Also struck by this curious Virgin over fifty years ago, Ludwig Bemelmans, in *The Donkey Inside*, tells that legend has it that the Virgin arrived one dark night riding a black burro. The burro pushed open the church door and walked up to the bell. Taking the cord in its teeth it rang and rang until the priest awoke.

He also mentions that the Franciscans tried opening a competing church to the original Dominican in Baños. The new church was a much fancier, imposing edifice with electric lights and an organ, however it lacked the Virgin everyone had grown fond of and soon folded it's altar wings and closed up shop.

In the town plaza, seven young men play Andean folk music. A guitar, *churango*, (a miniature mandolin made from an armadillo shell) and fiddle provide a bluegrass sound. A big skin and wood drum gives a primal pounding beat to the delicate notes of a wooden flute and pan pipes. The pan pipes of the Andes are thought to be the first musical scale instrument. One man shakes a string of hooves (pig? sheep?) adding a rattle rhythm. The drummer and flutist look like traditional Quichua, with a single long braid down the back, white pants, and fedora hat. The churango player wears a Harley-Davidson t-shirt and jeans. They're all having a great time dancing in a circle while they play and sing. Each instrument grows louder as it approaches me and then fades, except for the pervasive drum and the sharp notes of the flute floating clear and free above the earth bound musicians.

In front of the church across the street, the priest sprinkles holy water blessing an old pickup truck.

It has been raining in Baños for days. In this eight by ten room with a bare bulb hanging from the ceiling, I feel like I'm in a Beckett novel. I stare at the wooden door just beyond the foot of the bed.

Outside the streets glisten, water drips from the mountain sides. Clouds roll over the green mountains. Broken bits of blue sky promise little.

I don't know how people spend so much time traveling. I've only been gone a month and I'm already tired of it. Traveling alone, there's just too much time for thinking. There's also no one else to blame, no one else to get upset with. All this drifting through other people's lives, just looking in. All this transience seems so shallow. I'm failing Tourism.

What is traveling other than floating along from one place to the next? If I feel restless while traveling, I move on to the next locale. What about restlessness in one's own place? Does restlessness come from a lack of fulfillment? Is fulfillment necessary for the human spirit, or is it a disease? I feel like a shark who has to keep swimming to move water through its gills or it dies.

I keep going through these weird mood swings between hating this place, being depressed and wanting to go home and speak English, to having a great time and thinking about staying longer, surprising myself that I can carry on a conversation in Spanish.

The rains finally stop. The sun is out and there's a very sexy German girl in the room next door.

In a small bar that evening I play dice games with the German goddess and a Chinese Ecuadorian named Mario. Howlin' Wolf, Pink Floyd, and Tracy Chapman provide a welcome relief from "Rico-rico." The alcohol fails to lift me from melancholy, however, and I duck out early.

Baños—miracle hot springs that look and smell like runny mustard, a dopey virgin and constant rain. "It's fuckin' paradise, man," a friend had told me. I'm bored silly.

I take a spectacular bus ride to the nearby town of Rio Verde. Outside Baños, the road hugs a narrow shelf of mud; the Pastaza River roars far below. Waterfalls careen into the canyon. Thick green carpets canyon walls. On anything resembling a horizontal surface someone grows bananas, passionfruit and sugarcane. One fellow has his house perched high up the mountain. A steep trail zigzags down several hundred meters to the next somewhat level patch that is his garden.

In the tiny town of Rio Verde, the main occupation seems to be in the ramshackle log mills where they take nice logs and cut them into thin planks and cut these up to make crude wooden crates. The other primary occupation is mud.

I step over a pig squealing in the mud trying to reach his slop just out of reach of his short tether, and slosh through the mud and pig piss down a narrow trail.

A *campesina* and her small son collect guava fruits along the trail. They offer me a couple and show me how to eat the fruits. These semi-wild orchards provide much needed food and cash crops. Some people work so hard for so little. Who was it that was condemned to push a boulder up a hill for eternity?

The trail winds along a very bizarre cliff face. Pillars of columnar basalt rise from the base and twist and contort into a strawberry swirl of rock. Fractals on acid. James Gleick wrote, "...fractals flow toward infinity in a way that the mind has trouble conceiving."

I lay back on a rock at the edge of the river and watch the waterfall tumble down the opposite cliff. The sun warms my bones as the spray from the cascade blows back on my face. Water droplets slide off the cliff and tremble in the air. Chunks of water peel away from each other, then become a steady flow as gravity draws the molecules together again, reunited.

The cliff forms a sharp line against the blue sky. Black hawks soar on thermals against the green mountains. Returning to the solace of nature, I begin to feel much better. I spend over two hours watching the movement of the water and its performance with gravity, rock and air.

Downstream and high above, a tiny stooped woman leads a burro across a wooden suspension bridge.

On a Slow Bus to Jipijapa

> Clouds are not spheres, mountains are not cones, coast-lines are not circles, and bark is not smooth, nor does lightning travel in a straight line. —Benoit Mandelbrot

The place Britta recommended, Alandaluz, bills itself as an "ecological tourist center," which sounds like an intriguing juxtaposition, so I decide to visit to find out more and see the ocean. I've still got a couple weeks left in Ecuador, before heading to Peru and Bolivia. By keeping on the move, I can maintain the feeling that I'm not just killing time.

One catches the buses leaving Quito at the foreboding sounding *terminal terrestre*. Mortiz Thomsen relates the story Ecuadorians tell about bus drivers who run off the road and kill passengers without harming themselves. The driver must go into hiding to avoid revenge from the family of the deceased. It is rumored that whole villages in the Oriente are populated by bus drivers.

Some bus drivers instill confidence, or at least I try to think so, considering the next few hours of my life are entrusted to them. Other bus drivers don't. They turn up the radio, fondle girlfriends sitting behind them, scream at the passengers to move to the back, and try to make time, often simultaneously. The least inspiring, however, is the bus driver who stops at a shrine on the road to pray.

An old Ford truck, a big F-350, with a bus riveted to it provides the basic means of transportation. As many seats as possible are fastened to the bed and then encased in a sheet metal body.

A conductor, often a teenage boy, always accompanies the bus driver. The driver is the boss, but the conductor collects the fares. Somehow with all the stops and people getting on and off, he keeps track of who's going where, who's paid, and knows how much it is to each village. Sometimes I think he just makes it up. Occasionally the Indians and drunks who aren't going far don't get charged. The conductor helps load and unload passenger belongings from the roof of the bus, large sacks full of potatoes, clothes, shoes, car parts, and gringo backpacks with amazing rapidity. The conductor also yells out the destination with rhythmic volume, "Jip, Jipijapa, Jip, Jip, Jipijapa," trying to collect fares.

The driver and conductor keep a percentage of the fares, so they try to load the bus as full as possible and often won't leave the station until they've acquired enough passengers. The more runs you can get in the more money you make. In the land of *mañana*, the furious pace of the bus system adds a touch of irony.

Each of the colorful buses painted red, green, blue and white, has a name—Sangre de Toro, 22 de Julio, El Miligaro, Reina de la Camino, and Super Ford. In the 1930's the buses carried slightly different names: Hindenburg, Berlino, Zeppelin and Aldolfo Hitler.

The bus driver, a black man with sideburns, like he stepped off the Mod Squad, towers above Ecuadorians jostling to board. A shadowbox of the Virgin lit by a red Christmas light hangs above his head, next to it: a roadrunner cartoon sticker. A bumpersticker above the door proclaims "RADIO FREE CHINA." "*Dios es mi guia*" is painted in scroll letters on the rear of the bus. The salsa version of "Satisfaction" crackles the radio. Women climb on shouting "*Helados! Chicles! Mandarinas!*" Boys flash the latest headlines: "Murderer drinks victim's blood," "Two headed girl born." Photos of corpses parade under your nose.

The vendors pile off as the bus begins to move. Not inspiring any confidence, the conductor crosses himself as we ascend the steep, twisted road. The driver honks at campesinos and burros sitting in the road. Another bus coming from behind passes us. A competitive sort, the driver steps on the gas. The old school bus seats rattle loose as we bounce over bumps. Downhill, we gain slowly on the other bus. We begin to pass. A small, white car is coming from the other direction. The driver leans forward, and the passengers draw a collective breath. We squeeze by—two buses and a car on a slender road. We let out our breath, and we smile at each other.

The coast is almost a different world from the Andes. Outside Portoviejo, the capital of Manabi province, the bamboo huts grow farther apart. Building the bamboo huts on stilts allows fresh breezes from the sea to ventilate and also offers protection against floods. You can see the light steaming through the bamboo strip walls like those huts in the Vietnam movies. Great kapok trees dominate the sparse brown hills. The trunks swell at the middle, some bulbed and twisted, imbuing each tree with unique character. Few of the trees have leaves, naked except for the white and pink flowers which grace the branch tips. Unlike most trees, the leaves drop before flowering, exposing the flowers to bats for pollination. Dropping leaves may also help the tree rid itself of insects. From the bus window, the trunks and branches look green, like they're covered with algae. I want to worship them. In fact, the Maya believed souls ascended to heaven by the kapok.

I wonder why these trees, even more numerous than the tall cactus, are allowed to be so plentiful. Perhaps the wood is too hard to burn, or doesn't burn well. There are no stumps of the great trees in this ravaged landscape.

Later I discover the wood is actually very soft, but becomes brittle when dry, rendering it useless as timber. However, in the Caribbean, the trunks are hollowed out for canoes and coffins. The blossoms, on the other hand, soon yield a cotton-like substance which is gathered and used to stuff mattresses, upholstery, and life preservers, among other things. Coffins. Life preservers. Heaven.

The bus pulls into a gas station. The driver honks to get the goats to move out of the way. Wearing a dirty white blouse and shorts, an Inca princess boards the bus selling tortillas. She has straight black hair, and slightly oriental eyes and cheekbones. But it's her royal nose, sharp, defiant, and obvious like an isosceles triangle, that distinguishes her. I am spellbound. No buyers for her tortillas, she departs.

As we leave the gas station, an old Land Rover pulls in, roof stacked high with duffel bags and gear. There must be thirty people packed inside. Across the back window is spray painted "Jesus." There are no single occupant vehicles travelling the countryside.

The crowded bus smells of sweat and chickens. My head swims, and my heart aches. I think of home; even Quito has a comfortable familiarity. I want to tell the driver to stop, turn around, let me off. But I know I've gone too far.

A woman's chicken thrashes about. She quiets it by wringing its neck. The bus stops to pick up an old Indian woman, and lets off five drunks to piss.

At the bus station in Jipijapa hangs a framed poster of a good looking nun baring her chest to reveal a tattoo of Che Guevara.

I miss the last bus down the coast and ask the bus driver about finding a hotel. He says there are no hotels, but there are two *pensiones*. I walk a few blocks in the direction indicated and ask a woman sitting on the curb about finding a room. She gives me a curious look and nods her head toward a doorway. A boy comes running down the dark stairway, sees me and runs back up, returning with a large man in a dirty white undershirt, his belly bulging, and excited to show me a room. I follow him up the dark stairwell. In the dimly lit interior, I make out chicken wire cages delineating the rooms. He says to wait while he gets a key. The curb woman ascends the stairs arm in arm with a man walking unsteady, and they retreat into one of the cages. I don't think I want to stay here.

The other pension, a few blocks away, has one room left. A tiny, old man escorts me up the stairs to a clean, cinder block open air hallway. A couple dozen small red doors, about two feet wide by five feet high, line the blue plywood walls, each with a padlock. *Sure have a lot of storage here.* He unlocks a door.

I duck my head into the storage closet; the cinder block wall borders a bed on three sides. A bare bulb drops from the ceiling. I check the mattress for unwelcome guests and find that the mattress rests on pieces of cardboard. I've been sentenced to Jipijapa. All along the blue hall are tiny red doors, behind each, a bed.

I'm not quite ready for this, so I drop my pack and head toward the plaza to find something for dinner. The guide books say given an unknown, Chinese restaurants, one in every village, are a safe bet, as the food is always good and often the best in town. Jipijapa's *chifa* restaurant turns out to be between eatable and mediocre. It's also sweltering hot and the chifa's out of beer. I console myself with the knowledge that it's the best in town. A man comes out of the back to see what I want. There is nothing so lonely as being alone in a foreign country and the only person in a Chinese restaurant with dozens of red plastic tablecloths.

Searching for a beer, I pass the *Corazon de Jesus Farmiacia*. There's more *farmiacias*, at least two on every block, than bars, which are scattered rather thin. In the crowded pharmacies, abundant throughout Ecuador, you can buy just about anything without a prescription, which is nice if you're in need of Lomatil or Tylenol Three. Bristol-Myer advertising balloons and miniature blimps hang from ceilings. Over 90% of the pharmaceuticals come from multinational corporations, and a six million dollar subsidy from the government keeps prices low. However, the government recently announced it was canceling the subsidy. The effect upon people long dependent upon using powerful prescription drugs for any ailment is unknown.

Portoviejo, where I could have stayed, is reputedly full of beautiful women and music, and I'm here listening to latin disco and watching a couple of drunks argue on a Friday night. Jipijapa isn't even in the guide books. Once again I feel like I'm in a movie, except for that hotel cell looming over my consciousness, and I can't bear the prospect of sleeping there sober, so I guess it's *mas cerveza*. I wonder if Jipijapa is Quichua for "Hell."

It's too hot to sleep in the cinder block cell, so I walk up to the roof which contains a little garden patio with a hammock. I relax to the sound of mufflerless motorcycles and drunks until early morning, when the roosters begin.

Come morning, I catch the first bus out of Jipijapa and down the coast, rolling past small fishing villages. Along Machalilla National Park, the sparse vegetation changes to coastal dry forest.

A bamboo castle looms just above the beach looking like a set from Gilligan's Island. Palms and flowers flourish everywhere. Mangos droop from fruit trees. Ravel floats from the stereo. A fellow wiping off the picnic tables suggests I put my pack in the corner; breakfast is in a few minutes. Fruit, yogurt, granola, followed by a fried egg, bread and cheese and a delicious green juice that turns out to be alfalfa and passionfruit juice nearly erases the memory of the previous night.

After breakfast I set up my tent under a couple trees bearing white berries. The berries on the ground congeal on my sandals forming a thick paste. I find out later these berries are used to make glue. I move my tent.

Then it's down to the beach to dive in the ocean, warm enough to play in for hours. Walking along the beach, I run into Cathy from Minnesota who is in Ecuador conducting bean experiments with U.S. AID. We talk about soil and mycorrhizae and nitrogen fixation. Cathy is into Tarot and promises to give me a reading later. I return for lunch, vegetarian pizza and another tropical juice concoction. Everyone eats the same meal together fostering easy conversation between strangers.

"How long have you been here?" I ask Rob, a park ranger from New Zealand.

"I don't know," he answers in a slow, contented voice, "four or five days maybe."

"So, um, what's there to do around here?"

"Well, you make a dash for the hammock after lunch and then roll out for dinner."

A fully stocked bar makes me feel better about this low activity level. I could get used to it.

Waves crash on the beach, rolling a coconut shell split in two back and forth. A group of pelicans skim over the water like a squadron of B-52s with their huge wings, low slung bellies, and ponderous beaks. Three sandpipers run back and forth chased by the tide, probing the wet sand for tasty morsels. Hundreds of tiny crabs scamper sideways across the beach on invisible legs making the sand appear alive, pulsing with the tide. A couple wrapped in a blanket are the sole human occupants of the beach other than myself and the large Australian asleep in his hammock.

At the end of the long beach, frigatebirds ride thermals off the cliff, soaring above the outstretched arms of cactus. A sea cave hidden in the cliff face invites me in. Fish dart about in tidal pools. The cave goes in about fifteen meters. I grab the moist wall, feeling my way in the dark. Beneath my feet the ground moves. Hundreds of snails creep about, their shells small, black rocks in the sand. At the far end of the cave, jammed in place by the tide, lies a collection of wood resembling an alter.

The high tide pounds against the shore and crashes into spray against the rocks. Blues and oranges burst across the sky. A huge disk of orange sinks into the sea. I'm overcome with beauty. And, of course, I've forgotten my camera.

I awaken the following morning to a chorus of green parakeets darting among the trees outside the tent and walk out to the ocean for a morning swim. I return for a cup o' chlorophyll for breakfast.

A dozen of us staying at Alandaluz rent a boat to take us to Isla de la Plata, "the poor man's Galapagos." Not visible from shore it takes two hours in a long, wet boat ride to reach the small island, or a big rock, off Puerto Lopez. All of us get thoroughly soaked by the spray, a couple folks even shivering by the time we finally land. Sheer brown cliffs rise as we round the cape and pull into a cove. Half a dozen other boats lie tethered in the bay. A bamboo hut stands at one end of the beach. At the other is a white concrete structure drenched in graffiti.

Our trek begins as an organized tour but soon disintegrates. Cold and wet, the small boy with us doesn't feel like walking, so while waiting for that situation to resolve itself, Rob and his friend, Jennifer, walk on ahead with Carl, the Australian and his Irish buddy, Evan. I stop, take a few photos and find I'm walking along with Elizabeth, a Peruvian-Filipino woman from New York.

We climb a yellow-grey hill; below the ocean pounds against the little island. I wonder if this is volcanic, same as the Galapagos. I trudge along the island's rooftop. It's hotter than hell. Plant life is sparse. So much water all around and so dry. You'd think it would at least rain here. The dry gullies attest to that. But apparently the rains come strong and scarce, scouring away the dirt and pouring off into the sea before getting a chance to soak into the ground.

At the far end of the plateau, the land drops away. Our group scatters below across the dry plain. Sonja, the Israeli girl, sits in the scanty shade of a small tree. Carl and Evan come up behind me and plop their packs down.

"Care for a smoke, mate?" he says pulling a bong from his pack.

"You make that?"

"Nope, this American chap made it for me in Vilcabamba. This is a seed or a gourd and the bowl here is a nut. It's that real hard nut that they use in place of ivory."

"Tagua nut. They make buttons from it."

"Yeah, right."

Sonja packs up and heads down the trail.

"She's nice," says Carl.

"They're all nice."

"Yeah but she's got a couple o' real nice assets," he adds.

"What we need here is a couple of big iguanas," Carl points to the denuded hillside, "poking their heads up."

Suddenly the cactus and brush becomes intriguing and the ash grey dirt takes on new hues, and as we walk down the trail I drop back lost in my own mind. *This island's really a trip. So maybe I'll go to the Galapagos. I've always wanted to go. But it's so fucking expensive. What was it? $400 just for airfare and then you have to rent a boat and guide. I could do it though, go for a couple weeks, forget Peru and Bolivia and just go home.*

Suddenly, silhouetted against the sky, large birds circle just a few feet off the ground, big white-footed boobies, turkey vultures and higher up, the prehistoric shapes of frigatebirds. In front of me everyone has stopped. The trail goes right in front of a booby sitting on her nest. As people pass she reaches out, hisses and snaps her bill at the intruders. Why don't they just walk around her? It's not like there's a lot of heavy vegetation to fight.

Among the white blotches of booby shit covering the ground, several more nests next to another bush become apparent. It finally dawns on me we're in the middle of a rookery. The sky fills with soaring boobies, who don't seem greatly disturbed by our presence. While some species will abandon their nests if disturbed or swamp an invader, the boobies merely glide above, and soon after we stop, they begin to land and reclaim their nests. On such an island there are no terrestrial predators to fear.

We walk for nearly half a mile though the colony finding it difficult to avoid nests. You see a bird and walk around it and come up behind another. The booby paths and human paths merge and split a dozen different directions.

A nest of sticks placed in sort of a circle contains a single greenish mottled egg. Have the parents abandoned the nest, or are they just off getting a bite to eat? Wouldn't the egg fry, exposed to the direct sun? Wouldn't vultures snap up a booby egg?

In a bare patch sits a single boobie surrounded by seven vultures. I approach curious to see if the booby will leave the nest. As expected, the vultures fly off before I get within twenty meters. The booby sticks out her long neck clacking her bill at the departing vultures and stays put. The boobies don't leave the nest when approached even within a few feet. Why then the abandoned nest?

Occasionally trees, perhaps shrubs is a better word, crop up farther downslope. In a scraggly shrub five feet off the ground sits a pair of frigatebirds in their crude nest. One chick adorned in white down and the other in brown juvenile plumage shake and rattle their bright blue beaks at each other. This sibling discrepancy seems strange, however frigatebirds have one of the longest dependence periods in birds. Nestlings depend upon their parents for six months, and after fledging they are still fed by their mother for up to 14 months. Frigatebirds are also among the longest lived birds, living up to 34 years in the wild.

A few more juveniles, seven or eight, sit in trees surrounded by a colony of boobies. The boobies probably never encountered ground predators in their recent evolution and simply never developed complex nests. Furthermore, they breed on islands and rocks where trees are conspicuously absent. Frigatebirds are sea birds as well, so why do they nest in trees?

Weighing only two pounds, but with a six foot wing span, frigatebirds snag fish and squid from the water's surface, but are loath to enter the water, and have become adept at stealing food from other birds, diving upon them in mid air.

Along the cliff edge I come across Carl, Evan and Elizabeth overlooking the east end of the island. For a time we sit in silence watching the green waves crash on the black rocks far below. A different species of boobie, the blue-footed, float and weave on thermals. All three species of boobie nest on this island, the white-footed, the brown-footed and the blue-footed with their obscenely bright blue webbed feet.

"Well mates, I reckon we best head back," Carl announces.

By this time of day it's sweltering hot, and we're out of water. Taking a short cut back to the beach, we get lost in a tangle of brush and after fighting our way through, encounter a steep rock face which we slide and scramble down. An hour or so later, with sweat streaks down our dust covered faces, we arrive back at the now crowded beach and run into the ocean to cool off.

Carl asks the guy who's boat is hauled up on the beach if he's got any beer. Like a manna from heaven, he hands us a glass of beer with a couple of ice cubes in it.

Small watercraft, mostly green, open fishing boats like ours, some empty, some full of partying Ecuadorians, bob in the little harbor. Men play soccer on the beach. Seashells, bottle caps, and broken glass litter the front of the white bombed out looking building. Trash lies scattered about everywhere. Late on Sunday afternoon people fill the concrete shelter cooking on charcoal fires, eating and napping ,taking a cue from the brown boobies snoozing in the shade on a jutting rock at the end of the beach. Guys hang out on the beach, drinking and barbecuing. The smell of cooking meat and fish mixes with the salt air. There's something odd about this scene. Then it dawns on me. There are no women here.

The cooks at Alandaluz prove what can be done with the incredible variety of fruits and vegetables. The only problem is the Ecuadorian sized portions. Carl and I look longingly at others still eating their ratatouille. After a couple days of appetizing but unsatiating meals, we confront the manager, Nicola, who just arrived after a week's absence, with our hunger. Thereafter we receive heaping portions.

Visiting from New Zealand, Nicola Mears and her boyfriend stopped in Alandaluz two years ago and remained, growing vegetables and teaching organic gardening to local communities. Last year he contracted a rare form of malaria and died before they were able to reach the hospital in Quito. Nicola stayed on becoming manager of Alandaluz.

While the focus of Alandaluz is to provide a living example of organic agriculture and promote ecological awareness through community contact, tourism keeps dollars coming in. The private group which owns Alandaluz evolved specific objectives.

"The activities, buildings, and sources of building materials are developed in an ecologically sensitive manner," says Nicola.

Since Alandaluz is built from bamboo from the coastal highlands, and not much bamboo remains, a project has been implemented to replant nursery shoots of bamboo.

Nicola insists that the bamboo used for building is cut at certain moon cycles. "It's easier on the plant and lasts longer. But they need money, so they chop the whole lot down, eh? And it takes forever to regrow," she says. There is something magical about bamboo. This giant grass blooms at the same time all over the world.

Nicola tells me the children's projects have been very successful. Alandaluz offers art workshops, kids gardens, and vegetable growing courses for adults as well. Miguel, the chief gardener, shows me around the gardens. In summer they grow tomatoes, peppers, melons, and sweet potatoes. And in winter carrots, beets, leeks, and onions are raised. The vegetables are important in supplementing the local diet of rice, platano, fish, coffee and citrus, breaking the cycle of malnutrition. Since the land can be productive, the causes of malnutrition remain hidden.

In *Living Poor,* Mortiz Thomsen told of his first experience with the malnutrition spiral when he worked as a Peace Corps volunteer in a small village on the Ecuadorian coast. He expressed frustration at the laziness and lack of drive and initiative among the local people, until he realized, through adhering to the local diet, that one banana did not provide enough energy for a full day's work. He soon found he could only work for a few hours and just wanted to lie on his cot the rest of the day.

Miguel says he's going to Canada to plant trees to earn money to start another center like Alandaluz near Colorados, in northern Ecuador.

"Why is organic so important in Ecuador?" I ask Nicola.

"Organic agriculture improves diet and waste disposal, and breaks the financial and psychological dependence upon chemicals. Ecuador is the world's pesticide dumping ground," she replies. Although the use of DDT was banned in the United States in 1972, U.S. companies still manufacture and distribute DDT throughout the Third World. Chemical solutions to agricultural problems are highly encouraged and advertised by both the government and multinational corporations. Village walls serve as billboards advertising pesticides and herbicides.

The most impressive thing about Alandaluz is not the gardens, not the delicious food, not the beautiful uncrowded beaches, not the friendly eclectic mix of foreigners and Ecuadorians, artists and biologists, but the luxurious composting outhouses.

The nicest bathrooms in Ecuador are the only buildings at Alandaluz with a foundation. Stone work, bamboo, and a nice wooden seat give the small buildings a solid feel. A mix of sawdust, dirt and leaves keeps smell down. When one bin is filled, it lies dormant for a year while the other is used. Presently, tests are being conducted to see if the material will be safe for compost.

Such a simple solution to so many problems. Most of rural Ecuador lacks sewage disposal or even outhouses, which is why cholera is becoming epidemic. By simply teaching people to build outhouses you solve basic health and sanitation problems. By designing outhouses which compost human waste you provide a means to enrich the soil without becoming dependent upon costly and dangerous chemicals.

A shaggy white-haired bearded man with a small monkey on his shoulder and a crazed gleam in his eye strolls in while we are enjoying a beer after a hard day at the beach.

"Baooohaa!" he yodels and sticks out his hand.

His tan, bare belly hangs over his shorts which are about to slide off. Carl gives him a cool reception. He puts the monkey on the table. All the girls play with the squirrel monkey, and he snuggles up to them. Carl pushes the monkey away.

"Fucking monkey, always pisses on me."

The monkey runs around the table overturning coffee cups and saucers looking for sugar. Soon he spies flowers in a glass, yanks them out and knocks over the glass to get some water. Within twenty minutes the table is littered with ripped up flowers, overturned cups, beer bottles and monkey piss.

"Get your goddamned monkey off the table!" Monique screams discovering the mess. Monique is a little distraught at having monkey piss on the dining tables. Looking hurt, Baooha retrieves his monkey and ties it to a nearby post.

Forty-five years ago Baooha left Iceland, or was maybe thrown out, and has been surfacing throughout South America since. Carl first encountered him in Cuzco, Evan was stuck on a boat to the Galapagos with Baooha, and I'll run into him again in Quito.

Miguel says the nearest phone is in Korea, a small fishing village an hour down the coast by bus. I take a small journey to the village where the main occupation seems to be staring at the gringo walking down the wide dirt street. Three women of three generations sit on the porch of the house with the only phone in town. Pigs, turkeys, and geese fight for banana peels under the bamboo hut while one of the women nurses her baby. I give the matron the number and she goes through all the machinations of making a long distance phone call in Ecuador. After I finish the call, I give her the 1200 sucres she asks for.

Korea's main street ends at the beach. Several women and children dig in the sand with spoons. Wondering what they are digging for, I gaze around and see a bump in the sand and dig a clam-like mollusk out with my finger. As I walk along the tide flats I acquire a large handful of the shellfish. I return to the group digging, and smiling I drop my handful into one of their buckets.

In less than five minutes of casual picking I collected a good ten percent of what five of them had gathered after digging for some time. Why not just walk along and pop the little buggers out of the sand with a finger instead of sitting in one spot with a spoon? They don't seem to appreciate my contribution.

Fishermen walk through the surf with frame nets supported by a crossbar that they grab onto like a hang glider. Other fishermen carry small nets over their shoulders. I ask a man holding the fish bucket what they are fishing for.

"Lisa," he replies holding his hands about six inches apart to indicate the size of the fish.

Late afternoon beams of angled light bounce off the waves as the fishermen walk along the shore looking intently for jumping lisa. Taut, poised, they carefully sneak into the ocean, watching for where the fish may be. When one jumps, they quickly toss the net out to catch the unwary lisa. Mostly they come up empty.

Pelicans dive into the surf backlit by the setting sun as I return to Alandaluz for an undeserved dinner of shrimp crepes.

Carlos, the designated bartender, (he's the only one who knows how to mix drinks) brings me an Alandaluz, orange juice, tequila, something and something in a fruit shell. So the question of the day will go unanswered especially since Monique is baking pot cookies.

The chocolate sesame pot cookies are very good and potent. I wander out to the beach and listen to the waves roll back and forth inside my brain.

I return some time later to the dining area, and all the people sitting at the table have turned into dozens of huge toads hopping around under the bamboo shelter, big and fat from eating cockroaches. I figure I'd better return to the beach and my tent. The next morning I notice the lips of a toad poking out from a bamboo support in the bathroom. For a moment I think the hangover is worse than I thought. Peering again into the bamboo pole, a large toad stares back at me, sure enough.

I keep thinking hanging out on the beach in a comatose state is supposed to be fun, and something weird and interesting is going to happen, like I'm waiting for Hunter S. Thompson to show up or something. But he never does. I can't stand any more relaxation. Time to get out of here.

I'd better pack before the feeling fades. I pay Carlos my bill, $50 for six days of three meals a day and bar tab, and hitch a ride back to La Libertad and on to Vilcabamba.

"*Dios es mi copilito.*" A sticker with Jesus looking pious under a halo adorns the glove box of the old yellow gasoline tanker that stops to give me a ride.

We grind up the hill in first gear. Rococo, the driver tells me this is the road of five *cerros*, or hills. He ought to know, he hauls gasoline down this road from Jipijapa to La Libertad and back every day. I ask him how his job is.

"A bit tiring," he says.

Rococo speaks so fast and choppy I can hardly understand him. Driving along the cliff overlooking the Pacific Ocean, we talk about women. We talk about the Gulf War as the truck grinds through coastal forest. We talk about how much money a truck driver in the United States makes as we bump along dirt roads past bamboo huts.

Fireflies, Sunsets, and Cactus Juice

The ideal of the honourable man is expressed by the word *hombria*, "manliness"... It is a term which is constantly heard in the pueblo, and which the concept expressed as the physical sexual quintessence of the male (*cojones*). The contrary notion is conveyed by the adjective *manso* which means both tame and also castrated. —Julian Pitt-Rivers

At the bus station in Loja, so many people jam together at the door that new riders have to climb through the windows to board, barely leaving room to breathe inside the ancient pale blue school bus. The bus groans up hills in first gear and down in second. The brakes are shot. After a few miles of hairpin turns, it becomes apparent something is wrong with the bus. The driver has to back up to negotiate the tight turns; the wheels screech whenever he cranks the steering wheel. We can't quite make one turn, and everyone piles out. Women lead children down the ditch to pee. Some of the men stand around the front end of the bus, while others crawl under to investigate. The steering arm is broken, and this is the only bus for two days.

A half-hour discussion follows.

"No, that won't work."

"Do you have a jack?"

"Change the tire."

"Just keep going."

The driver produces a gigantic jack and somehow rigs a makeshift steering arm out of the jack handle. Everyone piles back on, and we're off at a fast crawl.

The world outside the window, however, compensates for everything. Cloud forests tumble down the emerald mountains, turning to *fincas* of coffee, corn and bananas. Adobe houses with red tile roofs sprout from the fields enveloped by gardens of papaya trees and flowers. Spaced well apart, the houses give each other plenty of room in the magical glow of late afternoon light. It's hard to think of this as poverty. These people have something—land—for which the truly impoverished can only wish, fight, or abandon hope.

People gradually filter off the bus as it winds up and down the dirt road. The bus lets me off outside the small village of Vilcabamba. I help a woman with a ponytail pull an ancient sewing machine from the roof of the bus. She's obviously not a tourist. I stand on the cobblestone street, wondering what to do next, as I watch the departing bus belch a cloud of exhaust.

A blond, very blue-eyed guy wearing welding goggles pulls up on a motorbike.

"Want to buy any San Pedro?" he asks.

"Jeff!" the woman exclaims in mock chagrin.

He looks at her as if to say, "What's the big deal, it's only some hippie."

The psychotropic cactus, San Pedro, may have been named after the belief that St. Peter holds the keys to heaven. Previously know as Huachuma, San Pedro probably predates Christianity. Pottery, dating back 3000 years, from the ancient Chavin culture depicts the tall, columnar cactus in association with jaguars.

Similar to peyote in that it contains mescaline, San Pedro is used by *curanderos* (healers) to diagnosis diseases, for divination, to own another's identity, and to communicate with the spirit world. After long night ceremonies, the *curandero* makes a dawn pilgrimage into the mountains to purify himself in the sacred lakes.

A *curandero* working with an American anthropologist said, "San Pedro has a special symbolism in *curanderismo*, for a reason: San Pedro is always in tune with the saints, with the powers of animals, of strong personages or beings, of serious beings, of beings that have supernatural power."

One early Spanish missionary demonized the effects of the cactus, "This is the plant with which the devil deceived the Indians... in their paganism, using it for their lies and superstitions… those who drink lose conscious-ness and remain as if dead; and it has even been seen that some have died because of the great frigidity to the brain. Transported by the drink, the Indians dreamed a thousand absurdities and believed them as if they were true."

I am most anxious to try it.

I walk into town to get lunch while Jeff heads to his stash. Two French girls sit at a table outside the corner restaurant with a bottle of Coke in front of them. They are laughing. Laughing so long and hard their faces turn red. Each dying gasp of giggle begins a new fit. A couple of local men keep trying to hit on them, walking back and forth in front of the women clicking and whistling and hooting. The men, not realizing they are the joke, keep parading, taking the laughter as flirtation.

"My friend's got some cabañas up in the mountains, you should come up there. Just ask for Charley's cabañas; it's up at the end of this road," Jeff says when he returns with a pint of brown liquid.

"Thanks, I may do that, but I told some friends I'd meet them at Madre Tierra."

As I hop off the back of Jeff's dirtbike, a young guy with long Robert Plant hair and a Greenpeace t-shirt struts across the terraced front lawn rimmed by orange and papaya trees. Flowers grace the stone balcony, and gardens peek from behind the house. Ducks and a couple of dogs bob around the yard. A girl in Birkenstocks lounges in a hammock. An Israeli with red dreadlocks plays pool on a miniature pool table with a flat-topped guy from NYC.

Madre Tierra overlooks the vibrant Valley of Longevity where people live well past one hundred years old. Only two other places have such a high incidence of longevity, the Abkhasians of Russia, and the Hunzas of Pakistan. All three communities survive in isolated mountain valleys.

Saturday night music drifts up from the village as I sit on the stone balcony watching the sunset and the full moon rise. Very peaceful, yet somehow the place exudes almost a—I don't know—forced casualness, like on the beach with everyone trying to look relaxed. I just got here, yet I feel restless. Am I a weirdo, a curmudgeon, because I feel a vague sense of discontent?

Hymie Mendoza, proprietor of Madre Tierra, sits like the Godfather at the breakfast table in his British racing car hat and sunglasses. To his guests, he explains yogurt as "Mohammed's milk, a beautiful bacteria." A green parrot walks around squawking underfoot.

Down by the river, a troupial, a large oriole with black spots on its wings, cackles. A rooster crows; a donkey bays. Across the bank, a couple of local kids bathe in the river. Israelis on San Pedro play cards in a cow pasture.

On the way into town, I stop by a bridge. It seems the whole town is gathered here to watch a race down the river. Some of the contestants float on inner tubes; others have small boats, some have paddles, some use their hands. Each is accompanied by a small group of boys howling encouragement. When someone overturns, the crowd yells and whistles. The river is so shallow, most of the boats scrape the bottom of the rocky channel. Some try desperately to stay in their craft, as if being separated by the river were grounds for disqualification. Others unabashedly pick up their inner tubes and carry them across the shallow stretches.

"Is that against the rules?" I ask someone.

"What rules?"

Indeed.

The last of the racers floats by. A couple of girls from Madre Tierra invite me to go swimming with them at the plush hotel pool down the road. Feeling unsociable, I decline and continue into town. Little red haired and blond kids sitting in the rusted-out bed of an old pickup pass by and continue up the only dirt road out of town. *I think that's where I need to go.*

Inquiring at the bakery, I find a man willing to take me up the road in his *caminoetta* to Charley's cabañas for two dollars.

"Why is this called the Valley of Longevity?" I ask as we bounce up the rutted road.

"*Es el climá.*"

"The climate?"

"*Sí, la climá es buena por la salud.*"

"How long do people live. . ."

"*Cein años, cein y vente años.*"

"One hundred and twenty years, really?"

"*Sí, verdad. Es la climá,*" he says waving at the verdant mountains.

He pulls to a stop where the dirt road narrows and becomes a path.

"*Las cabañas,*" he announces pointing to a bamboo gate. I thank him and swing the gate open into a garden of banana, coffee, papaya, orange trees, and flowers spread wide and red for a hovering hummingbird.

The *cabaña* sits by itself in the middle of the garden. Sugarcane and bamboo block the view from nearby houses. I walk up the trail past another *finca* or two, past a pig and into the orange trees and grass. It looks like this is the end of the houses.

Well, shit, it's such a nice day I'll just take my backpack and head up the valley and camp out. I have enough food to last a few days and there's oranges all over. I can keep going and sooner or later I'll come across something, a little village or something. "Con permiso donde estoy?" I'll ask some little old man and I'll have to figure out which way back to Loja. I'll hit something in a few days; this country is so populated.

What I hit was a raging river, a few cows, a couple of campesinos, and a trail that transformed into a jungle of flesh-ripping thorns.

In the States, when you hit the end of the road, that's it; it's the end of the road—no more houses, no more farms, no more people. How many people in the United States live in a place you can't drive to? Here you can walk for miles and suddenly come upon a house, a finca carved out of the hillside, a pasture, a man leading a burro loaded with wood. The roads through the Andes are ancient; a footpath is a road. It's all quite frustrating when looking for a nice wilderness backpacking trip.

I trudge back to the cabaña. The doors are padlocked. I'll have to go look for Charley if I want to stay here. I pick my way through the sugarcane to a clearing and climb up the hill. For the first time today the sun really comes out, and the valley bathes (I don't really like this word, but it works, so fuck it) in four o'clock light. The sunset is going to be awesome.

Below, a little girl plays in front of an old adobe house. I scramble down and walk through a wooden gate and across the bare dirt yard full of chickens. As I step up to the door, an old lady comes out wielding a machete nearly as big as herself. I ask where Charley lives, and she points across the narrow valley with the machete and mutters in toothless, incomprehensible Spanish. I nod and quickly back out.

Charley, 36, originally from New Hampshire, has lived in this valley for 13 years. One day he just quit his job, went traveling and ended up in Vilcabamba. He liked it so much he decided to stay and built a house on the hillside. The cabaña started as a guest cabin for friends.

He shows me around excitedly as if I'm the first person he's seen in weeks. He pulls a hammock from one of the rooms and hangs it across the patio. The cabaña even has a kitchen! A Coleman stove, a bucket sink, a few dishes, pots and pans, and instant coffee. But it's a kitchen, nonetheless. Around back is the shower. "We just put this in. Be careful with this," he says showing me how to light the propane hot water heater mounted on the wall. "You have to light it before you turn it on, otherwise it'll blow up.

We don't have hot water up at the house. I hope you don't mind if we come down and take showers."

"No, of course not."

"The outhouse is down that path," he vaguely waves toward the garden.

"You need anything? I go into town pretty much every day. You need anything, you let me know." Charley pulls a notepad from the kitchen cupboard. "Just write down whatever you want and leave it on the table. Beer?"

"Oh yeah, I could use a few beers."

"Okay, well just leave a list in the morning. How 'bout San Pedro?"

"I got some from this blond guy on a motorcycle."

"Oh, yeah, Jeff. He lives right below me. He said he'd met you. Wanna smoke some pot?"

"Sure."

"I mean, I wasn't sure, you know? If that was cool, right?" he says running his hand through his thinning hair.

Charley finally sits down on the bench at the table, but with one leg on the outside, in case he needs to flee at any moment.

"My inlaws are here, so I can't smoke at the house, right?" he says pulling out his stash.

"The longest I was away from the U.S. was six years, that's a long time. What tripped me out the most was those magnetic price bars you see in the grocery stores. I always figured they were for inventory. Oh, and in McDonalds they have those cash registers where you just hit "Big Mac" or if you want four catsups, you know, *puttdoiing*—four catsups. That and a plastic card that you can get money in the grocery stores. And there's hot showers."

I suspect Charley would probably have already had several heart attacks if he lived anywhere other than this *tranquillo* valley.

"Here, I'll just leave this with you." He hands me his stash and pipe. "Let me know if you run out. I mean keep it cool, right? Most people around don't give a shit. Sergio, he's really the only one who will smoke," Charley says and hurries back up the hill. Whew.

I pick an orange off the ground and climb the pole ladder to the small second story deck to sit and watch the sunset and eat the sweetest, juiciest oranges in the world. Chickens cluck and scratch amongst the sugarcane. Crickets provide chorus to the river's background melody. No people noises, no cars, no salsa music blaring from scratchy speakers, no roosters (although I'm sure the old lady with the machete has roosters), no voices from the street. Fireflies glow on and off amongst the bananas, and a full moon rises above the Valley of Longevity. I may never leave.

The next day Sergio stops by and shows me around the garden. *"Siga no mas,"* he waves at the garden imploring me to take whatever I wish. I'm beginning to figure out what this strange expression unique to Ecuador, *siga no mas,* means. Literally, "follow no more," *siga no mas* can mean "keep going," "don't worry," "have no concern," and "move to the back of the bus."

Sergio shows me a *tomate de arbol* tree and asks if I want any. Sure. And do you want a papaya? Sure! A few minutes later he returns with four *tomates de arbol* and a good sized papaya, five pounds maybe, all for twenty cents.

I climb up the hill in back to a grassy point at the end of the jutting finger of Loma Cucharillo. The ridge stretches east ten kilometers to Cerro Solomanca at 3700 meters (11,800 feet), a green, jagged promontory occasionally visible through the clouds. While nearby hillsides stand bare, cleared for firewood and cow pasture, thick vegetation carpets the peaks. Silvery blue leaves of cecropia trees lining the *quebradas* breaks the green. These trees are distinguishable even from across the valley by their huge pewter leaves, eight to twelve inches across and much more functional than the biblical fig leaf. The trunk of the cecropia is thin and grey, the leaves sparse, two or three per branch. Their scarcity adds impressiveness, each leaf worthy of hours of contemplation.

With binoculars I can see the silver ribbon of a waterfall spilling out of a lake nestled in a cirque between Cerro Solomanca and the next peak. Beyond the peaks is unknown, presumably more mountains, before plunging into the Amazon basin with nothing but rainforest for hundreds of miles. The lake looks beautiful, a pure, unspoiled blue, a place I desperately wish to get into. *It shouldn't be too tough, just follow the ridge to Cerro Solomanca, bag the peak and drop into the crater. Give it a try in the next day or so.*

These mountains form the backbone of Podocarpus National Park. In the United States, a National Park suggests Winnebagos, park rangers, trash cans, slide shows, traffic jams. However, in Ecuador, a National Park only exists in the most remote places, not yet trampled by campesinos and recreationists.

Podocarpus is named after the native conifer, once extensive, but because of heavy exploitation is only found in inaccessible areas. The podocarpus has been largely replaced by Caribbean pine and eucalyptus, the latter introduced because it grows very rapidly and can be cut down sooner for wood.

Directly below me the eucalyptus forest tumbles toward the valley. Behind me grows one of those mesquite-like trees. A couple of giant prickly pears with trunks like trees rise fifteen feet high. Lichen grows on the trunks, testifying to the age of these cacti. Huge pads, ten inches by six inches, spread skyward like the paws of a praying bear.

While the mountains seem perpetually shrouded in clouds, the Valley of Longevity and the western cordillera blush in the setting sun. As I put on my sunglasses to sit back and watch the show, a man comes down the path below me. *I'll just make myself invisible.* But a few minutes later he walks into my little spot. I figure he just wants to watch the sunset too, but he's checking to see who I am. His family walks by here every night on the way home from their fields. He points to a house far below. He thought I was a robber or someone going to jump them. We both laugh at that and sit and talk while the sun sets.

"Must be a long walk to work every day," I say.

"Not if you're used to it. It's good for the health."

He tells me his name but I immediately forget it. It's about two pages long, and he says it very fast. Anyway, he's 24 years old and a senior in high school. Not because he's stupid, he tells me. He has to work all the time, so it takes a while to get through school.

Today is the celebration of San Pedro. I stop by Charley's to get specific directions to the waterfall he recommends. Good thing, because it lies two *quebradas* beyond where I thought.

"Ok, see that tree," Charley says, pointing at a lone pine on a distant ridge. "That's a good place to sit and hang. There's a hole up there where they used to bury people—no, it's cool—back before the Spanish. The Spanish dug it all up looking for treasure. So anyway, there's a hole there and just beyond is the waterfall. It looks like it drops right off, but there might be a way down to it."

Climbing past the fields of cane and banana, I'm soon on the ridge looking down into the next valley. The trail is so eroded, ten feet below the surface in places, that it seems like a tunnel.

From the ridgetop the trail stops climbing and contours the mountain. The drainage with the waterfall is still a ways off. *Let's see, if this takes about a half hour or so to kick in, I should just be getting near there. How strong can it be, I mean it's organic, right?*

I sit on a rock and pour out a dose of the sticky brown liquid, which everyone says is foul tasting. *OK, plug the nose and slam it. YECHH! That's the worst tasting shit—enough to make you barf right there.* But I down it in one shot which is the only way to do it because you'll never get your body to accept it if you hesitate or try and sip it. I follow with a half quart of *agua.*

The trail leads through a crude bamboo gate which I swing open and enter the Realm of San Pedro.

About a hundred meters down the trail, the cactus kicks in. *I'd better get to that waterfall so I can sit down.* The trail winds through a cow pasture, along a fence, past a house, a corn field, through some trees, and over a creek. I pick up my pace. *Oh, oh.* Walking becomes difficult... my heart pounds. There's the tree, fifty meters straight up. *Deep breath, here we go.* Climbing to the tree, sweat pours off me; my heart races. I collapse. Cow shit everywhere. The valley spreads out below. Four campesinos work the opposite hillside, clearing the forest for cow pasture. *I wonder why they left this tree standing.* A rock crouches about ten meters above me. *Yeah, the rock, if I can just reach that rock. A rock would be good.* I sit at the rock awhile. Below, a stream runs through a small clearing surrounded by trees, and in the middle of the clearing sits what looks like a stone bench. *I wonder what that is? Wow, Charley's built a bench for tripping. There's no way I can take out my binoculars; I can barely focus as it is. Okay—I'd better make it down there while I can.*

Somehow I find myself in the pleasant clearing with a nice creek running through it; the waterfall tumbles below. *Shit, here's the trail. I don't want to be near a trail.* The bench transforms into a water trough. But I can't go any farther, so I find a grassy spot and flop down. Little annoying black flies are everywhere, black dots zigzagging in front of my eyes. *Lots of bugs. Oh well, they don't seem to be biting, except there's a cut on my leg.* I squash them. *Hope they're not laying eggs or anything gross like that.* Better not think about it. I'm sitting in a cloud of mosquitoes. *Sunglasses! that's what I need. I'll just look past them.* Put on the sunglasses and the bugs vanish. Some other bug lands on my arm and draws blood. I kill it, but it doesn't matter. *It doesn't bother me so why worry? So what is there to worry about? The sun's coming out and baking my skull, but it's okay. I mean I'm not hungry so why worry about food, of course, you'd die, but why worry about death, I mean it's inevitable.* I look over my shoulder. *Death is always over your shoulder, looming back there. I'll look Death straight on.* I turn around. But it's still over my shoulder.

I watch the clouds spin and curl in their kaleidoscope patterns. *I mean*

*look at these patterns, everything twisting around on itself; the world is cyclical,
I mean the Hindu are into that—reincarnation—so why does Death matter?*
I begin to soar. My body becomes red, intently glowing like fire. The
sun comes out from behind a cloud. The red explodes into yellow, then
green, and I'm away, free-floating through the universe. *What if I don't
come back?* And I open my eyes. The growing, twirling wisps of clouds race
over the mountain top. The sun casts a red tint to the kaleidoscope, and
the clouds form into stylized Mayan Jaguars. I close my eyes. Jaguar appears. I go off again, transforming into Jaguarman. Yellow head, huge
teeth dripping with blood. I'm hungry. Ravishing. I want meat! *Yech,
blood.* Jaguarman explodes into a field of soft red, blooms into yellow, then
pink like a time lapse flower opening. And it's—it's—a Flamingo! Its tail
spreads like a magenta peacock. It turns its head and smiles a dopey smile
like only a flamingo can and flies away. *My totem animal is a flamingo?*

I wish it would rain… and it begins to rain. *What if you were so in tune
with things that you could feel something as it was about to happen or before it
happened and thought you caused it to happen? It's easy to see how some Inca
king tripping his brains out would believe he's child of the sun and all. But then
you could get rid of bugs. But then if the bugs don't bother you ….*

*Lots of visuals, oops not supposed to get caught up in visuals. Those are
witches, says Don Juan. That would be weird, tripping with some 80-year-old
Indian. That would be cool though, having a San Pedro spiritual guide—then
again I'd probably just laugh and say leave me alone, rather than get caught up
in witches and spirits and things. What if spirits are only real because we've
evolved into thinking along those lines? Like time. We can only understand
time linearly. Oh sure, I know time isn't linear, but tomorrow is still after
today. I'll never be able to get around that, so I can never truly understand
time. But then everything gets older, and then I guess it dies, cycles, repeating
patterns that are never exactly the same. Just like the kaleidoscope clouds.*

An old man, about 125 years old, walks by. Very slowly. I close my
eyes and vanish in a flash of red. Yellow light shimmers where my body
once was.

The sun pounds down, so I move into the shade, and for the first time
I notice cows grazing on the hillside above. I drift down to the creek thinking how nice it would be to splash water on my face, and I see the creek has
been trampled by cows—the banks churned into a muddy goo. I look
around and realize I've been sitting in a cow pasture surrounded by cow
shit.

*If nothing matters and everything is cyclical then why worry about these
cows; I mean what difference does environmental destruction make if we are*

part of nature and the whole cycle of being, if our causing mass extinctions is part of a natural process? The clouds build and gather force over the nearby peaks.

But we've removed ourselves from the cycle. And here's these damn cows. Cows may even be more disgusting than people. Of course the Hindus worship cows. Perhaps there's a modesty factor at work here; worship a lowly god, humility and all. People are considered sacred too. Cows and People, what could be more un-godlike?

Okay, I've got to get out of this fucking cow pasture. Struggling to my feet, I wander around trying to make a decision. All I really want to do is sit down again. I manage to take a leak. *Glowing piss, highly hallucinogenic, should save it.*

Following a cow trail, I finally make it up the creek a few hundred yards. Lots of trees and lianas and vines—very jungley and dark. Farther up the creek a small waterfall cascades just visible beyond the vines and greenery. Now I know why everyone always carries a machete. I Indiana Jones my way through the plants and spiderwebs.

The place is literally crawling with life. I try looking at a spider mummifying some insect but can't focus, so I gaze at a cecropia leaf for awhile. *And what about spirits? Are they real or did we make them up? Are spirits just a manifestation of human perception? Is there such a thing as a water spirit?* I ask the waterfall. *Is there a spider spirit?* I ask the giant spider above my head. It doesn't answer.

I climb out of the jungle into the cow pasture—a whole hillside of cut and burned stumps and scrubby undergrowth. I slip and slide on the damp black earth like a cow plodding along.

The sun begins to set, turning the clouds pink. Not quite prepared to walk, I sit down again. *There's a full moon tonight; I can walk back in the moonlight!* As it grows darker I look back—no moon rising. *Shit. It's be-hind the mountain.* So I put my legs into drive and hurry back down the trail in twilight. By the time I reach the Portal of San Pedro and the ridge, it is night. But poking above the mountain is the full moon so bright it hurts my eyes to look straight at it. Venus is also very bright. At least I think it's Venus. This is the Southern Hemisphere after all. With all the different stars, I could be on a different planet. Except for the cows.

Under the rising moon, the wind blows a cloud into being. Thin wisps grow out of the dark sky, twisting and folding into a grey cloud which soon blocks the moon. Still, some light seeps through, and I pick my way down the trail. Sweating as I come off the ridge, I feel the wet heat rising off the valley to greet me. A dog barks, sounds of kids and roosters. Lights.

At the cabaña I light a candle—can't handle the bright electric light—and peel an orange. Then a piece of bread. *Might as well try one of these tomato de arbol. I wonder how you eat it.* With my knife I peel the hard shell of skin revealing a fleshy orange tomato with hundreds of seeds. At first it tastes like a fruit, rather sweet and tart, but just when you decide it's a fruit, it tastes like V-8 juice. Pretty tasty once you get over the surprise. I down four of the plum-sized fruits and start eyeing the papaya. *I wonder if I can eat a whole papaya.* Very ripe and juicy. Delicious and messy, just what I want. I eat about half the papaya followed by a few Oreos for dessert. I drag out my sleeping bag and kick back in the hammock to watch the moon and clouds drift along the ridge.

I spend the morning watching the rain drip off the garden. Staring at a coffee plant while drinking instant coffee, I wonder why the closer you get to coffee, the worst it tastes. It's virtually impossible to find real coffee in Ecuador. All the coffee is exported, corrupted into instant and shipped back. When you ask for coffee at a restaurant you can expect a warm cup of water and a jar of freeze-dried, if you are lucky. If you are unlucky you get *esencia,* which is not espresso, but rather coffee boiled down to a thick concentrate, of which you pour a thimbleful into your cup of warm water. This addiction of mine has helped precipitate a condition where people grow coffee for export instead of corn for consumption.

In this not very well tended garden, the path to the gate bursts with color from myriad flowers. Large fuchsia composites, the flowers so massive they droop toward the ground pulling the plant earthward, stand sentry near the cabaña. Impatiens sport orange and white petals like high school cheerleaders. A fern yields its lacy fronds to a nasty looking thorny plant with tiny orange flowers. A delicate, four petaled purple flower, each petal like a tiny propeller, neighbors a large white lily. Yarrow thrives amongst succulents. Ten-foot-high woody shrubs with red tubular blossoms, the sort of flowers for which hummingbirds are designed, line the fence by the gate.

Ecuador yields more plant species than any other country. And these valleys at the edge of the Andes in Southern Ecuador are internationally renowned for their diversity of plant life. Especially fruits.

Bananas dominate the garden. I never knew bananas grew upside down. I guess I never really thought about it before. From a thick stem, a large, red cone, just beginning to open, hangs below the banana bunch. The cone is composed of leaves which peel back like an artichoke. As each leaf peels off, it reveals small, yellow flowers.

Interspersed among the bananas are coffee plants, the green beans just turning maroon. Next to the nearest coffee plant, pinky-finger-sized peppers dangle like Christmas ornaments from the Aji tree. Aji is the Ecuadorian version of the jalapeño, although not nearly as tasty. Here and there is an occasional papaya tree. At the far end of the cabaña an orange tree drops its fruit. A young tomato de arbol raises its large figlike leaves at the turn to the outhouse. Below the garden lies a field of bamboo used for building. A wild fig spreads its branches over the river, its ancient trunk covered with lichen. Bromeliads grow in the crook of the fig's limbs. Cherimoya grows on the hillside above. The ugly grapefruit-sized fruit can be broken open and the milky white fruit scraped out. Some people like cherimoya. Maybe I just ate too many.

Sergio walks by bearing an armload of yuca tubers. He gives me one, shows me a nearby lime tree, a coma tree (some bizarre fruit), and an *achiote* tree with spiny seed pods. The red achiote seeds are ground into a face paint by various tribes. He points to an avocado tree, but it's not in season. Next to it stands a lima tree or "sweet lime." The fruit has very strong citrus odor and tastes like a bland orange; it's very good. The lima tree is his father's. "So don't take too many; a few is okay," he says.

I ask Charley about a plant that looks like marijuana I'd seen growing on hillsides. "It's yuca. Everyone eats it. It's like potatoes in Ireland." He holds his hand out four feet above the ground, "When it's about so high, they cut two sticks off and stick them in the ground and they branch off. It takes about eight months to a year to grow. They grow a lot of it."

The tuber's skin peels right off, revealing a fibrous white substance. I boil the eighteen inch yuca for about an hour. It definitely tastes like a tuber. Yuca, also know as manioc and cassava, can be pounded into a flour or, as is common in Ecuador, boiled like a potato and served with rice and chicken, or rice and beef, or rice and pork. Elsewhere, yuca is made into tapioca. Yuca has been under cultivation for so long that it no longer grows wild.

In less fertile soils yuca contains high concentrations of cyanide to protect the tuber's rich food source from subterranean insects. Because of this defense, yuca is one of the few crops which grow in poor soil. However, the root must be vigorously washed free of the cyanide.

The Huaorani and other Indians of the Oriente tell of the myth of Mani. The unmarried daughter of a chief became pregnant, and against his condemnation, insisted she was still a virgin. Nine months later she gave birth to a white baby girl causing great excitement among the tribes. The infant was named Mani and appeared healthy and vigorous, however a year later she suddenly died. She was buried according to custom, and her grave was well watered and tended. After some time a plant previously unknown sprouted, grew and fruited. Birds eating the fruit became intoxicated and this increased the mystery surrounding the plant. When it finally withered, they dug it up and discovered a tuber resembling the body of Mani. The tuber became *Mani oca* which means transformation of Mani.

Charley hands me a *zapote*—a softball-sized fruit with brown skin and bright orange meat. It tastes like sort of a cross between a mango and a sweet potato. We then split a *guaba*—like a giant bean pod; the white silky meat surrounds a large hard seed.

Charley and Sarah made *humitas* last night, sort of a tamale.

"Here's six; we figured maybe a 1000," (one dollar) he says, handing me a loaded bong made from bamboo. "You know they had these on Gilligan's Island. They just didn't show that part on T.V."

Charley wants to promote tourism. "Groups, horseback rides, that sort of thing, and feed them."

"Aren't you worried about that ruining your life-style?"

"Yeah, but I need to make money," he runs his fingers through his hair. "As long as we get the right sort of people. As long as we don't get any of those hippies."

I must look surprised.

"I don't mean, you know, people that are cool about it, right? I mean those hippie types that hang out in groups. They do the San Pedro and just sit there. They're kinda young, know what I mean?"

"In June and July it will pick up; 'course there's the cholera thing. I can't say I blame people. I mean, I wouldn't want to go to a place that had cholera, right?"

Charley suddenly realizes he has lost his watch. He figures he left it at the cabaña, so he asks Sergio, who is taking a couple of burros laden with adobe bricks, to look for it. Sergio is building a small house near the cabaña for himself and his bride. Sergio comes back—it's not there. Charley starts freaking out. "Shit! Where's my watch? I know I took it off when I took a shower. It's got to be down there somewhere. Did you see it."

Shit, I hope he doesn't think I took it. "No."

"I'd better go look for it."

At the cabaña, Charley's watch is not to be found. So he scoots back up the trail to his place. A few minutes later I drop into the hammock and there's his watch. I figure I'll take it up later when I go watch the sunset. *He'd sure like to have it. Maybe I can catch him.* I walk down the path and there's Sergio. I hand him the watch thinking he's on his way back up the hill for another burro-load of bricks.

But what IF HE'S NOT? Have I just assumed the role of white master to the brown peasant? Am I the hacienda owner lounging around in his hammock while the serfs dig tubers and lug burros through the muck? I hope he doesn't think I assumed that he'd trot his little self up the hill. Shit.

But wait. There's the burros plodding back up the hill, Sergio behind them casually swatting one with a small branch. The motion so halfhearted I doubt the burro even feels it.

A sheet of rain blankets the valley; even the ground under the big banana leaves is wet. Jeff comes by the cabaña to see how the San Pedro went. He talks about the *paramo*, "The weather that comes down from the Andes, up in Podocarpus—it rains like hell. There's some good sized peaks up there, 3500 meters, but you've got to be lucky because the paramo comes in without warning. Last year three people died up there." Paramo refers not only to the high elevation grasslands, but also to the furious storms that sweep through the Andes.

I asked Jeff how he ended up here.

"I was going to school in Northern California and my girlfriend and I spent two months looking for housing and school started and it rained and we had no place to live so I went to school for two days and said 'Fuck it.' So I went up to Oregon to plant trees and it rained for two weeks and they said vegetarians get sick from planting trees. I'd better eat meat 'cause they sprayed the areas to plant with 2,4,5-T to keep down the weeds, and vegetarians got skin problems and sick. Well shit, it didn't matter if I was a vegetarian or not, I wasn't going to work there. Well, I went back to Santa Cruz and studied organic agriculture for a while and I read about Ecuador. I figured the tropics, why not? Jim and Barbara who were on the farm down here said it's great, there's pineapples, and hummingbirds feeding off the pineapples like paradise. What they didn't mention was that the pineapples had spines on them."

Jeff, who's a fruitarian, moved here eight years ago, for the abundance of fruit. Like Charley, Jeff spoke no Spanish when he first arrived in Ecuador. He continues, "They didn't say anything about visas and amoebas. But I love it here. I've got land and can grow stuff. Where could I have land in the States? And there's no winter. I like that."

Jeff recently married a Vilcabamba woman.

"My wife's great-grandfather lived to 121 and her great aunt is 116. There's a lot of people over 100 for the amount of people who live here, right?" he says.

Baptismal records and charting families support the claims of people being 110, 127, and even 132 years old. In 1971, Vilcabamba had nine centenarians out of a population of 819, representing a rate of 1100 per 100,000 compared to the U.S. rate of 3 per 100,000.

Not only do they live to be more than 100, they have the minds and bodies of people in their 60's and 70's, reported a team of doctors. *Los viejos* don't suffer from modern ailments such as heart disease, arthritis, or broken bones. In the few instances of heart disease, the symptoms were not felt and treatment was not required.

"There used to be a lot of old people in this valley. Lots of fruit, good climate, clean water. But now they take a pill instead of a bunch of herbs. They die sooner," Jeff states.

Four U.S. expatriate families live at the end of this small valley: Charley and Sarah, Marta and Glen and their kids, Barbara and her kids, Jeff and Maria. Like all immigrants, they left their homeland to find a better life. They discovered a place where they can be part of a community and lead a simple life on a piece of land without being hassled by taxes, rent, cars, pollution, police, gang wars, and other conveniences of modern life. All live in one or two room houses they've built; none have running water. They grow most of their food, or buy from neighbors. They're trying to build a paradise, rejecting consumer values and removing themselves from the world's insanity.

I could be part of this community, hang out, eat fruit all year, do San Pedro, but I know I won't. I want to settle down, stay put, but I still feel restless. I feel this need to climb mountains, explore valleys. The Denver Post used to have a quote from Harold Bonfils below its masthead, "*There is no hope for the satisfied man.*" I stared at that every day for ten years. I am still not sure what it means.

Jeff mentions that Marta is baking bread that afternoon and I should head over before it's all gone.

Marta is in the midst of paying her workers for the week, factoring in the tomatoes and cheese they brought her. Marta and her workers make a seasoning salt which is sold in Quito. After the women leave, Marta tells me their husbands don't really like their wives working for her since she once gave them all a beer after work. I can picture the five women sitting around surreptitiously sharing a beer in the safety of Marta's kitchen late one Friday afternoon. This Friday however, they collect their wages and hurry home to turn the cash over to their husbands so they can get drunk all weekend.

"Someone found out they had a beer and told the rest of the men, so they all got drunk and came home and beat the women," says Marta.

"Why?"

"Women aren't supposed to drink."

"Wait a sec. The men get drunk and beat their wives for having a beer?"

"It's machismo—one guy beats his wife and the rest have to do the same to prove their manliness if you don't want your drinking buddies to pick on you. It's fucked."

Glen walks in. Glen is grumpy in paradise.

"Glen works all day at the village water house. Building it. He comes home in a bad mood," says Marta. A Swiss company plans to bottle Vilcabamba mineral water for export.

Fifteen years ago, Marta came down from the United States for a six-month vacation in South America. She met Glen in Columbia, and they decided to buy land in Ecuador.

"First we rented a place back aways, then the owner thought we'd try and claim the land. So we bought this piece and built a house. That burned down four years ago."

In addition to the whole wheat bread, which had just come out of the oven, Marta has dried bananas, granola, and healthy brownie bars. As I load up on supplies for my trip into Podocarpus, four, five, maybe six kids, some brown, some blond, spill in. Spanish and English mix together and subside when they see a stranger sitting in the house. Finding what they are looking for, they rush out and down the hill. Four of the kids, one an adopted local girl, belong to Marta and Glen.

Although electricity came to Vilcabamba in 1975, this valley didn't get it until a few years ago.

"When we first got electricity, I didn't even want it but now I couldn't live without it," Marta said pulling a rack of bananas from the oven.

"Not much changed, except people had refrigerators and could have *helados* and medicines and stayed up later. A lot of *farmacias* came about that time. The old people suddenly had antibiotics and started dying. I'm sure it's just a coincidence, right?"

"Last month Barbara's mom came down for a visit. She was here about three days and freaked out. She said, 'I'd sell my house to charter a plane out of here.' She just couldn't take it."

"Why not? What's so stressful about here?" I ask.

"She's an American," Marta answers.

I climb the ridge and hike past the waterfall to scout a route into Podocarpus. I surprise a falcon sitting on a rock. It takes off, so I commandeer the view. I look up the Rio Yambala to the green mountains of Podocarpus and stare hard at the opposite ridge. *I'd sure like to get in there, climb one of those peaks. It looks like you could hike along that ridge, would be the way to do it. Getting up there would be easy—about five miles right along the ridge. Take about three days, do some exploring. Get into that crater for sure.*

A woodcutter coming down the mountain breaks my daydream. He leads five burros, each dragging two rough hewn eight-foot planks on each side. Hugo, the woodcutter, stops to chat as his burros methodically tromp down the trail. Hugo started out from his house at four this morning. It is now ten. He'll come back up after lunch and spend the night in a shelter and take another load down in the morning.

"That's a long day."

Hugo shrugs.

It's no wonder these people live to be 120, cruising up and down these mountains all day like they're walking to Seven-Eleven. Of course I know people who won't even do that, but start up their cars to drive two blocks.

Humans are adapted for long periods of exercise. Our species spent thousands of years walking ten, twelve, hours a day. The Tarahumara Indians of Northern Mexico hunt by running down deer. They chase the deer until the prey drops from exhaustion. They do this barefoot. The Tarahumara were invited to participate in the 1968 Olympics in Mexico City. However, when they arrived, they were disqualified because they would not wear shoes.

Our legs are the strongest part of our bodies, yet they are immobile most of the day. A friend of mine works in a nursing home where people sit around waiting to die. There are no nursing homes in Vilcabamba.

While genetics might play a role in longevity, life-style appears to be a greater factor. But there must be something more than simply a diet of fruit, vegetables, grains, plenty of exercise, a beautiful climate, and a low stress life-style. Is it the curanderos, the San Pedro? Everything grows healthy in this valley; witness the vitality and diversity of the plants. Is there some geophysical phenomena we have yet to detect that makes this valley unique? Why do certain places invoke spiritual stirrings?

Hugo says when they cut down the trees, they plant seeds so new ones will grow. I sure hope so. I want to ask him more, but I can't find the words in Spanish for "sustainable forestry practices," and his burros are far down the trail.

Charley, his wife Sarah, and her parents, visiting from England, are sitting down for an afternoon snack of some fresh squeezed orange juice and pound cake when I stop by to ask about possible routes into the mountains. We sit at the picnic table on the patio watching the rain. There are no chairs inside the bedroom/living room/ kitchen. Between bites of cake, I motion toward a large plastic cistern and ask about their water supply. The water comes from a tank filled by a river upstream.

"Pressure is a bit of a problem," Sarah says in typical British understatement.

A man arrives soaking wet with two sacks of corn looped over his shoulders like saddlebags. He has walked for two hours in the pouring rain, the corn loaded on a horse, to make the delivery. Charley buys all sixty-five ears of corn for 2500 sucres ($2.50). Four hours round-trip, plus the time and energy to plant and grow and harvest the corn for less than four cents per ear. He would feed his family on this?

The farmer informs us that the fiesta will be on Saturday. That's when summer arrives, and it stops raining. Charley says the fiestas change, no fixed dates, but they always mark a change in the weather.

"They can look at the sky and tell a year in advance what the weather's going to be like and set the date for the fiesta. For the past four years or so, the weather's been real screwy. This fellow says three more days of rain."

I stand to leave.

"Take some oranges; make some juice." Charley waves at a fifty-pound sack full of oranges. "Take twenty or thirty. Takes a lot of oranges to make juice."

Although the man with the corn said three more days of rain and then summer, I'm determined to get into Podocarpus today, to the valley with the lake. I pack my gear and head out early.

The weather does not look good; it rains off and on all day. After following the ridge for miles, the trail suddenly drops down to the Rio Yambala. The rust colored clay is slicker than snake snot. And I land hard every time I slip and fall.

The thigh deep river rages, swollen from the storm. *Okay, its just a river—you can cross it.* On the other side the trail disappears in a steep, rocky hillside covered with large, woody plants with shark-tooth-sized thorns which tear holes in my Gore-tex and leave deep gashes in my hands when I grab a plant to keep from sliding down the muddy scree. I fight my way up, figuring the trail <u>must</u> be up here somewhere. Higher I climb, through the thorns and slipping backwards through the mud, until I run up against a small cliff.

Just when I think it can't possibly rain any harder, the rain increases. Jeff's words from the previous day come back to me, "The lake spirits don't like people to go up there, and they make storms to drive people back."

I slip and slide down the muddy slope back through the fearful thorns. Maybe the trail goes along the river. *I've been in this damn country two months, and I still haven't summitted any mountains. A snowstorm on Cotopaxi I can understand; that's almost excusable, but rain? You're not going to let a little rain defeat you?*

There's no trail along the river, either. I stand at the edge of the rising river, weighing my options. The vegetation is too thick to bushwhack near the river, above are mud, thorns and a cliff. There's beer at the cabaña.

By the time I make it back to the lower valley, the sun is beaming down, the peak is poking out from behind the clouds and a hummingbird is sucking nectar from the yellow flowers of a banana tree.

Jeff stands in his kitchen grinding up cactus in a blender when I stop in the next day to inquire about a better route into the mountains.

"You need to go up the next hill before dropping down to the river," he says when I explain my foiled attempt.

"Oh."

The blended cactus looks like guacamole. Or a frog. A bagful of cactus skins lies on the table. Long strips of green cactus, like snake skins, are spread across the counter with holes cut out where the spines should be.

"You got to take off all the spines and around them. That's got strychnine," Jeff says.

"You just use the skin?"

"Yeah, the green is where the mescaline is. I only take the ones with seven sides."

"How come?"

"I don't know. That's what the herb doctors say, so I do it. One time I got one with six sides. It was at night. I went to get some under the full moon, and it was on this cliff, so I had to lean way out and lop off a branch and let it fall where my girlfriend could pick it up. We got back to the house to cook it up and she said it only had six sides. You could hardly see it, much less count how many sides it had. It was okay, but it wasn't as good as the seven sided. Some have five sides, some eight. I've never seen a nine sided cactus."

"Why do you cook it? Can't you just eat it?"

"Try it."

I take a piece, chop off a tiny bit.

"It's pretty bad."

"Each bite gets worse," says Jeff.

I could see that. You can down one cup of juice once in a while, but it would be pretty hard to eat much cactus.

"How much of this is a hit?"

"Well, let's see, you need about this much," he holds his finger and thumb fully extended apart, "all around the cactus, so with seven sides." Jeff pulls out a strip and measures seven finger-thumb lengths and holds it up. It's about one and a half inches wide and fourteen inches long. "This would be a hit."

Jeff lines up the remaining strips of cactus and begins chopping. "I don't take any of the ones around here. There's so few left. People come in and they want some cactus so they cut the whole thing down. It takes a couple hundred years for them to grow. Or people hack at it with a machete. I try to take the parts that have already been hacked at or trim them where it's getting crowded so another can grow. Then I always plant the top in a hole about this wide," he spreads his arms apart. "Then that sends out shoots. It's weird."

"I don't get mine around here. I go way over," he adds.

Jeff dumps the blender of green goo into a big clay pot, one of those Saturday market museum imitations. I forget, they're not imitation; they are real.

Jeff cooks the cactus over an open fire outside for two days. "I know people who use the big aluminum pots, but I'd rather do it in clay. It's better that way."

Barbara drops by with Jeff's daughter and her son. She sits on a cushioned bench and prattles on, shifting back and forth from English to Spanish. The kids seem to have such freedom, wandering around from house to house. Of course, there's no traffic to worry about, just muddy trails and burro shit.

Dennis, who owns Jeff's house, arrives unexpectedly. In contrast to Jeff's sandals and cutoffs, and Barbara's overalls, Dennis and his friend look like they just stepped off the plane from Miami. He wears nice jeans, a belt, flowered shirt tucked in, sunglasses, and a gold chain. She sits quietly, like she's on display in her short skirt, high heels, and low slung tight blouse. So many women in Ecuador wear clothes that look like Barbie doll accessories. It seems odd that they dress like prostitutes in this conservative Catholic society where women live with their parents until they're married.

Now living in the states, Dennis is here for a couple weeks. There is something oddly familiar about Dennis. He talks fast and can't sit still.

Dennis tells us about his friend, Francisco, who was smuggling a suitcase full of cocaine. At Guayaquil everyone had to get off the plane before it left the country so the dogs could check the luggage for drugs. The police were training a new dog and had planted a bag with coke amongst the passenger luggage. The dog went straight to Francisco's suitcase. "No, no," the police insisted and pulled the dog to the "correct" bag. When they released the dog, he went straight for the "wrong" suitcase again. The police pulled him over to the planted bag once more. Again the dog went for Francisco's bag. Exasperated, the police gave up on their new dog and let everyone back on the plane.

When Dennis and his friend depart as suddenly as they arrived, Barbara asks, "Are the police still looking for Dennis?"

Jeff nods.

"How did he even get into the country? I mean it's pretty risky, right?"

"He makes a lot of money. He's just got to meet up with a few collectors, set up some contacts, ship the orchids up to the greenhouses in the states. It's pretty lax."

"Orchids?" I ask.

"Yeah. Dennis smuggles orchids. I don't really approve of it. Some of those plants are pretty rare. People pay a lot of money for them, right?"

"Orchids?"

That evening, Marta and Barbara invite me to accompany them to the fiesta. We stop by a small, blue house to meet Mama Elena and her four daughters who are also going to the fiesta. Mama Elena shares her house with her daughters, her three grandchildren and one son-in-law, raising the children while the women work at Marta's. Besides the kitchen there is a bedroom, a back room and a living room with a bed.

Three of the women are single mothers. Marta explains how men charm the young women making all sorts of promises. The girls fall in love, get pregnant, and the men dump them. The logic of machismo makes this acceptable: the more women you can knock up and dump, the greater your virility.

Bad salsa music blares from the loud speakers set up in the school yard. Most of the men are completely plowed by the time we get there. I bring everyone, except for Marta and Barbara who are already ahead of me in line, a big cup of beer. The daughters sip the beer surreptitiously and hand it back to Mama. She is so small and old, yet such a presence. When she laughs her wrinkled face breaks into hundreds of little smiles.

The fiesta to mark the end of the rainy season soon turns into little more than a drunken high school dance.

A small, black and white dog hangs around the cabaña. One night I give him some leftover rice I can't finish. I know I shouldn't, but he looks like he's starving. His ribs are sticking out, and I was going to throw the rice out anyway. No sense letting it go to waste. No sooner do I set down the bowl than another starving dog shows up. This one laden with puppies. *Christ. Now I'll have to feed the whole damn countryside.*

The guidebooks say not to make friends with any dogs in Ecuador because you'll never get rid of them, and besides they're disease ridden. "It creates a dependence."

The next night there aren't any leftovers from the scrambled eggs and the dog (I refuse to give him a name) just stares at me. *He's not my dog. I'm just passing through.* But he's starving, so I give him a piece of bread. The dog has an infected wound on his hip and can barely walk. He keeps licking the pancake sized lesion. He's going to die soon, but keeps hanging on. He even tries to follow me on a hike but only makes it a few hundred meters before turning back. What's he going to do when I leave?

I now make twice as much pasta as I know I'll eat and give the leftovers to the little dog. I can't just let him starve. Even if he is going to die soon from the infection anyway. It is certainly no sacrifice for me to feed the dog. It's certainly no great sacrifice for me to give a quarter to every beggar I encounter in Quito, but I don't.

The longer I'm here, the more I understand my country. The United States was settled by the peasants of the world. It's really just a rich Third World country. People are still hung up on acquisition, consumerism, hard work, a better life for their children. For a people who have eaten potatoes for generations, our standard of living is new and frightfully tenuous. Someone might try and take it away from us. Is this why we are so fearful of poverty? Many nations are terminally infected with poverty, debt, drought, corruption. Is it really a sacrifice for the United States to feed the starving? Or does it create a dependence, like the guidebooks say?

Three German dudes show up at the cabañas one morning, suddenly interrupting my tranquility. At least I can practice my Spanish as they don't speak much English. For some reason German Spanish is easier for me to understand than Ecuadorian Spanish.

The Germans split a dose three ways. They are concerned about doing it the first time, they keep asking about *Paranoia.* "Germans are like that," says Jeff, "Some are so uptight, they always seem worried about paranoia. I don't know if it's the way they're brought up or the Hitler thing, or what."

How can they be so emphatically self-righteous, telling me the United States is fucked up and imperialistic? They say the oil fires in Kuwait are the fault of the United States and point at me, like I'm somehow personally responsible for U.S. foreign policy. I don't judge people by the politics of their government, so why do people, especially Germans, think I'm representative of the U.S. government? I suddenly turn defensive and patriotic.

"Have you been to the U.S.?" I ask.

"Oh, sure, L.A. and New York."

"Most of the U.S. is between L.A. and New York."

"Oh, we drove across all that."

"Yeah. It's flat."

"I'm sorry you missed it," I say.

"There are people living in the streets," they accuse.

No shit. You think I don't know that?

"Does Germany have a solution for homelessness?"

No? then shut up.

It hasn't rained since the festival on Saturday. The man with the corn was well tuned to the weather. It's a clear warm day, blue sky and feeling like summer, so I attempt another climb into Podocarpus. With an early start I should be able to walk the ridge to Cerro Solomanca and drop into the valley with the lake, and maybe if it's hot enough, go for a swim in its pristine waters.

Charley suggested another route than crossing the river. "Take a left at the big orange tree and go up." When I reach the top of the ridge, the small path disappears in the thick head-high bushes. I realize I've forgotten the one thing a stroll in Ecuador requires—a machete. If a trail ever existed, the vegetation has reclaimed it. I'm sure it doesn't take long with all this rain. I follow a likely looking ridgeline. A faint path enters a patch of second growth, winds through the trees and diverges into several capillaries. I follow the more frequently used route, climbing over downed trees, around lianas and through undergrowth. The foliage gets thicker, and I can no longer see the sky. I turn and go up a hill; the gaps in vegetation dictate the course. I look behind me. I can't tell where I've come from. I look in front. I can't find a clear trail, just game paths leading everywhere and nowhere. I try to retrace my route, and everything looks strange. I stop and turn around thinking I'll head back up, and I can't tell where I just walked. *Shit.* I fight my way to where it looks like a clearing. There's a clearing all right but the mountain drops down; it doesn't look like there's any ground under all that grass. I edge out on a fallen tree. The sun's blaring down; sweat runs down my face; branches are stuck in my hair. I retreat back into the cool forest. *Better sit down. Drink some water and think about this.* I look for a place to sit. Everything is green and covered with plant life, insects, spiders, and who knows what. *Oh, well.* I flop down on a bed of moss and stare at the bromeliads hanging in the branches. *Sure hope there's no snakes here.* I stretch out on the moss. After awhile, I gather myself up and pick my way back through the forest to the ridge. I had a feeling I wasn't going to make it into Podocarpus, so I brought some cactus juice along just in case.

As the afternoon clouds over, the swallows zoom in snapping up insects. The wind whooshes through their wings as they drop out of the sky. I open my eyes and watch them swoop. High above, across a patch of blue, soars a zone-tailed hawk. *Yeah, a hawk, or even a vulture. A condor, yeah. One. Two flaps and just cruise. Except you have to eat dead meat. Wouldn't be so bad, I suppose you'd get used to it.* I close my eyes and listen to the bugs again. *Or a bat, that would be cool, dart around. I wonder what that would be like—seeing by sonar?* I try to locate the bugs as they zip past. *You could hear landscapes and rocks and bushes, everything.*

I gaze around at the ferns and swallows and hundreds of insects and at the denuded hillsides. *Humanity oozes up the mountains, into the rainforest, spreading disease and pestilence and cows wherever it goes. People are just bugs scurrying around trying to get everything they can before some other bug comes along.*

Is reducing the population anti-evolutionary? Is that going against a natural compulsion. Why haven't other species fucked up the planet? Can we consciously change our own evolution?

But wouldn't that be removing ourselves further from nature? Remove ourselves from nature. A world without people. That's an environmental utopia.

Would people be willing to gradually die out? Go extinct? Most people think humans are more important than the land. A world without people—no books, no art, no music—but aren't these all ultimately human attempts to mimic nature? What about Hope, Ideas, Creativity? Are these purely human traits? Will George Bush and the power structure willingly give up their golf carts for redwoods? Will he give up his tanks and jets? Will Americans give up Las Vegas and let it sink back into the sands for a few desert tortoise? Will John P. Jones give up his car for a forest? Will Hernandez Mendosa give up his firewood for a podocarpus? Will people stop having children? Would I get a vasectomy?

The world standard of living is increasing while the quality of life is decreasing. How do you measure TV against clean air? How to get people to deal with the earth on it's own terms, rather than imposed. How about zero tolerance for human caused extinctions? What would happen if we put monies for the drug war into habitat and species and preservation?

We don't need to suck all the oil from the ground. Now there's a male occupation—plunge a pipe down into the ground, find the hidden gold at all costs and suck it dry. Is it too late? Nature is pretty strong. We are like an adolescent boy rebelling against his mother. I hope we grow out of it.

And how do you keep environmentalism from becoming dogma? Without guilt. Guilt produces resentment and righteousness. But there's still the "I know I'm right, and you should listen to me." Instead of banging away at the fortress let's sit back, have a smoke and see if there is another way, or just leave it alone. Agriculture seemed a big step in the wrong direction, that and city states and civilization. We obviously can't go back in time, but maybe we can dance around this rock face and find another route.

Maybe there's something to this whole pinnacleness. I mean what's the point of climbing the mountain? To get to the top, right? The world is rounded, not pointed, so wouldn't it make sense and harmony to make a circle? To walk around the mountain.

I lay back in the grass and ferns and watch flight. The air fills with insects: flies, bees, butterflies, dragonflies, beetles. There must be over a hundred species of insects streaking around me. Two tiny flies dance and hum above me. A third joins in, and they circle higher and higher, then dive back down. One lands on my knee. I reach out unthinking and squash it.

A butterfly alights on my outstretched hand. Being ever so still I raise my hand, bringing it up for a closer look. The butterfly intently licks my finger with its proboscis, which is yellow and feels sticky. I can't tell if it's goo or a tiny barb on the end of its tongue. The tip fits neatly into the crack in the skin of my finger. It's going after the orange juice on my fingers. Why would I kill a fly and leave a butterfly unmolested?

The butterfly on my finger has charcoal wings with a black crust along the edges, a black fuzzy body and concentric rings for eyes. I stare into the insect's eyes. I see nothing. A rhino-like horn sprouts from its forehead. Not a terribly aesthetic insect when you look close. Just another bug.

I close my eyes and listen to the buzzing and flying. A cloud transforms into a naked woman on a white horse. She is part of the animal, sinking into and blending with the horse and then rising out of it. She emerges and changes shape like she's creating herself—or hatching—until she turns into a woman. The horse rises up, sprouts wings and we fly away.

Indians and Oil Companies

The governor, General Miguel Marino Torralvo, issues the order for the oil companies operating on the Colombian coast. *The Indians do not exist,* the governor certifies before a notary and witnesses. Three years ago, Law No. 1905/55, approved in Bogotá by the National Congress, established that Indians did not exist in San Andrés de Sotavento and other Indian communities where oil had suddenly spurted from the ground. Now the governor merely confirms the law. If the Indians existed, they would be illegal. Thus they are consigned to the cemetery or exile. —Eduardo Galeano

My plane for Lima, Peru leaves in a couple days. The arrival of the Germans reminds me I'm still a visitor and had better be on my way. However, I don't feel ready to leave Ecuador. I no longer feel compelled to keep moving. But this is supposed to be an adventure, I keep telling myself. Weary of the gringo trail, I'm unsure of what I'm doing. I'm tired of witnessing the world as if it were in a glass cage.

I miss my flight to Lima because of a four hour breakfast with Britta at Quito's Hotel Oro Verde. The breakfast buffet overflows with pancakes, eggs cooked any way you like, trays of fruits and pastries, everything. Except seafood. We arrive before eight and finally leave very satiated after noon. I can't bring myself to actually get up and leave her sitting there. And I haven't even packed yet. I guess I won't be leaving Ecuador today, so we spend the rest of the day walking through Quito. As we stroll down Amazonas Avenue, a.k.a. Gringo Alley, the shoeshine boys come running up to us. *Oh no.* I cringe. *Here we go again. I hate this.* This time they don't ask for money or shoeshines, but come to greet their friend. She knows most by name and asks how they're doing, engaging them.

One of the most aggressive hustlers, an older boy with a withered arm, is especially happy to see Britta. She introduces me to Ricardo. All the times I've seen him, all the times I've held up the same pair of ratty tennis shoes refusing a shoe shine, I never thought to ask his *name.*

On Sunday afternoon, the Parque de las Carolinas teems with kids playing soccer, none with a real soccer ball. Anything from a small, hard rubber ball to a beach ball will do, so long as it's round. Everyone plays, Mom, Dad, kids from two on up. If they can walk, they play soccer.

Lovers, families, and friends paddle around the canal in little boats. The balloon man crosses the bridge; yellow, blue, green, red and purple balloons float above his head. Quichua women in long dresses and derby hats sell salted and barbecue flavor banana chips, Coke in plastic bags, candy and oranges. A man leads his son on horseback through the park. Street urchins in torn clothes wade in the fountain under the bronze condor. Boys with homemade kites run past a clown and his puppet announcing the next show. Lovers kiss and draw apart. German shepherds in obedience class argue pointedly, while a tall, blond woman stands beside her Great Dane. All the dogs in the park are purebred; their owners carry leashes.

On the far side of the park a huge concrete cross looms behind a stage set up for a free concert. A hang glider dangles high against the green peaks of Pichincha.

One girl wears a t-shirt depicting a skull wearing a green beret and a big knife through his head and saying "Kill 'em all and let God sort them out."

Three giggly teenage girls rudely bump into a young Indian hauling two crates of Coke to a vender and nearly knock him over. The girls frown at him in disdain, and he looks at the ground in apology. This white/dark class distinction is so pervasive it seems unconscious and an established part of behavior. White equals money and power, European, beauty, the standard. Dark means poor. Indian.

Why am I still not excited about travelling on to Peru and Bolivia? I feel I need to quit wandering around aimlessly and <u>do</u> something. With the extra few days I have from missing my flight, I wish to learn more about what's happening with petroleum development in the rainforest. Searching the files at the South American Explorers Club, I find thousands of reports on climbing mountains but only a thin, dated file on Ecuadorian environmental groups.

At La Casona, I share a room with Larry, who recently quit his job as a management consultant in Los Angeles and is in Ecuador researching sustainable products from the rainforest. It always distresses me to see someone so young carrying a briefcase, but he's made a brave move. I meet Kevin who's also concerned about what's happening in the rainforest, and he suggests I get in touch with Paul Dulin of CARE International.

In his busy downtown office, Paul takes time out to explain the two pristine areas under immediate threat of petroleum development—blocks 16 and 22 (see maps). Both blocks include large parts of Yasuni National Park and the Huaorani Territory and are under concession lease to Conoco, a subsidiary of DuPont.

In 1979 Ecuador created the Yasuni National Park in the heart of the Oriente. Shortly thereafter, a consortium of oil companies led by Conoco discovered oil in the park. In the spring of 1990, the government of Ecuador, in a thinly veiled political move, expanded the neighboring Huaorani indigenous territory to 1.5 million acres. Much of this land resulted from redrawing the boundary of the park to exclude the proposed oil fields, which now lie in the deepest part of the Huaorani territory. However, the government did not give the Huaorani any mineral rights.

"The government comes off as concerned by giving the Huaorani territory," says Paul.

Although petroleum exploration and development are illegal in national parks, "The law of hydrocarbons supersedes all others. This country's government is famous for subverting its own legal instruments," says Paul.

"The government views oil as in the best interests of the country and actively encourages development," he continues.

Paul points out that Conoco, while not having a proven track record, has been fairly conscientious. Exploration is generally localized and takes place by river or helicopter.

"There's minimal site disturbance—three to fifteen acres. Regeneration is quite quick," he says.

However, seismic cable lines require swathes five to ten meters wide through the rainforest every mile. "Obviously this impacts wildlife, but mostly from noise disturbance from the explosives," Paul adds.

Conoco has repeatedly pledged publicly to conduct petroleum activities in an "environmentally sensitive" manner. For example, they promise to use cluster wellheads, drilling wells angling in from one site, rather than drilling numerous sites. They also promise to rehabilitate the area and not interfere with the Huaorani life-style.

In blocks 16 and 22, about 125 Huaorani (out of 1200) live a traditional hunter/gatherer life-style. Semi-nomadic, they live in family groups of fifteen to twenty, subsisting off monkeys, *javelinas*, small garden plots, and their incredible knowledge of medicinal plants.

Paul informs me that the Huaorani are just starting to organize, but it's difficult after years of traditionally fighting each other. Not only do bands like the Tangeri attack outsiders, intertribal warfare is common.

"These guys go in and raid this village and take the women, a very warrior-like people," Paul says.

The Huaorani don't believe in natural death, but view death as a consequence, usually caused by a *brujo* of a neighboring clan. A death in one's tribe calls for revenge. Traditionally, forty percent of Huaorani deaths come from revenge killings.

This intertribal violence serves an ecological purpose, keeping the Huaorani widespread so as not to deplete forest resources. However, the missionary Summer Institute of Linguistics persuaded several Huaorani tribes to settle in villages, with the resulting environmental deterioration. The missionaries also imposed their morality and discouraged native celebrations. As a side effect of this cultural disruption, anthropologist Laura Rival states, "Parents have notably more children today than before."

And in *In the Rainforest*, Catherine Caufield writes, "One of the most important adaptations forest people make to their environment is limiting the size and density of their populations to the level the ecosystem can sustain. If a group is below a certain size, for example, various infectious agents, including those that cause mumps, measles, and influenza, will not be able to survive. There are many ways of controlling population size, including regulating the age of marriage, sexual taboos, contraception, abortion, infanticide, death penalties, warfare, and abandoning the ill. Population density is regulated by warfare, limits on the size of extended families, and other, more abstract cultural values, such as a desire for freedom and a fear of outsiders."

The oil companies also contribute to Huaorani settlement. PetroCanada relocated the Babeiri tribe near the oil road. "The Huaorani have accumulated pots, t-shirts, plates, tapes, pocket lights, and spoons; in the meantime, they have been selling all their game to the military and oil workers. Their diet has worsened: sugar, rice, coffee, canned tuna. The children do not go to school, nor into the forest for that matter; they spend their days watching oil trucks and military vans passing by," writes Rival.

The Huaorani do not distinguish between the fifty different oil companies; they simply refer to them as "the company." They view "the com-

pany" as another forest resource to be harvested. There is no word in Huaorani for work, but rather a repertoire of words meaning "making" or "doing." They refer to cutting seismic trails as "busy land doing in the company."

"The company" employs Huaorani men to cut the paths for seismic
lines and in return provides the workers and their families with food, pots,
clothes, tools.

According to Rival, traditionally, sexual division of labor was minimal
and "not sustained by any ideological representation of male dominance."
Now ninety percent of the men have worked for the oil companies. "The
sexual division of labor is today a reality, as most men work in the oil companies and as women do most of the agricultural work." When the men
leave the village to work for the oil companies it creates a disparity between
men and women's experiences. "They learn how to be Ecuadorians, they
learn Spanish and they acquire new habits and values."

In block 16 lie an estimated 250-500 million barrels of oil. To access
this pool of dinosaur goo, a ninety mile road and pipeline must be built
into the heart of the Huaorani territory. The new road will open the area to
colonization, further eroding the Huaorani culture, as well as clearing the
forest to raise coffee, bananas, and cattle. ELF, a French company which
holds the concession north of block 16, has already constructed fifteen miles
of road.

To prevent colonization, Conoco and the government agree to police
the road, and not build a bridge across the Napo River; the pipeline will go
under the river. However, after the twenty years for which Conoco holds
the lease, the title reverts to the government, which views the Oriente as a
release valve for population pressure. As long as land can be opened up in
the Oriente, the government will diffuse the land distribution struggle by
building a bridge and opening the road to colonization.

For nearly 20 years, international oil companies, led by Texaco, have
sucked oil from a vast reserve near the headwaters of the Amazon. So far,
oil roads have opened 2.5 million acres of rainforest. Slicing though what
was recently pristine rainforest inhabited only by the Huaorani, the sixty-
three mile Via Acua, the road running south from Coca to the Shiripuno
River, now supports a population of 30,000 colonists.

The oil companies maintain that colonists destroy the rainforest, not
petroleum. However, as two rainforest ecologists note, "To blame coloniz-
ing peasants for uprooting tribal people and burning the rainforest is tanta-
mount to blaming soldiers for causing war."

Rival points out that most colonists are actually oil workers who do a bit of agriculture or supply oil workers with the necessities of civilization—bars, brothels, stores, and labor. "Without oil companies, there would be simply no colonists living down the Via Acua," she writes.

Paul contrasts Conoco to "Texaco which is one of the worst polluters in developing countries and in the United States as well. They have no safeguards. They were the first and cast the model for petroleum exploration. Braspetro (a Brazilian company) is horrific and ELF is no better."

Admittedly Conoco is more susceptible to environmental pressure than, say, Petroecuador or Braspetro; it has a public image to maintain.

Paul points out that "if we succeed in stopping Conoco, the government opens the lands to concession, and Braspetro most likely goes in. Conoco can be held accountable for environmental safeguards. I'm not supporting Conoco." Paul stresses that in no way is he in favor of Conoco; he's just recognizing the political realities of the situation.

"What's Ecuador's biggest environmental problem?" I ask.

"The government," he replies without hesitating. Paul says he's worked all over Latin America and this is the worst he's ever seen. "Not just the current government, it's the whole way it's set up. A new government comes in and says now it's our turn to get rich."

Some of Ecuador's "political realities:"

* Up to its volcanos in debt, Ecuador is highly dependent upon petroleum exports, which account for 40% of the nation's income.

* From 1972 to 1982 the government earned over $7 billion in oil revenues.

* "15% of Ecuador's rainforest has been destroyed by oil production, which entirely depends on foreign investment," states Laura Rival.

* The failure of land reforms can be traced back to the World Bank and International Monetary Fund for instituting policies and pressures on Third World countries to cut social services and food programs to service their debt.

* The World Bank is considering a $100 million loan to Ecuador to develop petroleum reserves.

Back at La Casona, Larry's on his way to meet with Douglas Ferguson of the Rainforest Information Centre (RIC) to discuss sustainable products. I tag along to the RIC house, just a few blocks away. On the way, we run into Kevin who's just come from there and is quite excited. Apparently, the RIC is heading into the Oriente for three weeks to work with the Huaorani, and Kevin will be joining them.

"Cool! Do they need any more help?" I ask.

I didn't want to go to Peru, anyway.

"I don't know, man. They're a weird bunch," he warns us.

Douglas is an arrogant, rude, unfriendly, paranoid, chain smoking Australian. I think we'll get along just fine. Larry introduces me as a graduate student/park ranger, which I immediately sense is the wrong move. Larry wants to export chrigra bags and hopes Douglas can set him up with the Huaorani.

Chrigras are the original "shopping bag" of the indigenous people of the rainforest. Light, durable and amazingly strong, these hand woven bags are used by the Huaorani, Shuar and other tribes to carry fruit, vegetables, fish, gear, anything, through the dense forest leaving both hands free.

Larry believes chrigras are a sustainable product that directly contributes to the economic well-being of indigenous people without sacrificing their culture. Rather than becoming oil or construction workers or languishing in the cities, many indigenous tribes can support their culture and life-style by making and selling chrigras and other *artisina*. One adult will take more than a month to make the expandable fish-net-like bags, which are woven or knotted from the fibers of the chambira palm.

They make the chrigras from the fronds of the palm thus not fatally damaging the tree. Douglas says there's no danger of overexploiting the palms as there are tons of palms, lots of jungle and few Huaorani. It's hoped the increased travel and contact from the chrigra business will aid in the communities becoming politically organized. Only through organization will they be able to hold off colonization and development.

While Douglas and Larry are discussing chrigras, I ask Sparrow, an energetic ethnobotanist and junior shaman, about participating in the upcoming Huaorani project. I'm not even sure exactly what it is they are doing—something like cutting a boundary around the Huaorani territory. At first, Sparrow doesn't seem too enthusiastic about me volunteering.

"The Huaorani eat monkeys. So you better be able to eat monkey meat," Sparrow says trying to discourage or test me. "It's a lot of hard work, swinging a machete all day cutting line," he adds.

A blond kid sitting next to Sparrow looks at his hand which is black surrounding a stitched gash running the length of his palm.

"Luke nearly lost his hand," says Sparrow.

"I fell on my machete."

"And some crazed Huaorani shot at him the first time we went out."

"They blowgun monkeys out of trees, man."

Luke, barely 19, spent two four-week stints with the Huaorani.

Douglas is asking Larry for $2000 up front. Larry insists he's exploring options, but wants to work through the indigenous federation. A bit unprepared for this unbusinesslike approach and talk of financial commitment, Larry departs.

"Out there in the jungle, I'm the boss. What I say goes, no questions," Douglas tells me before ducking into the office to agonize over strange messages on the computer screen.

"You know anything about computers?" he asks poking his head out.

"A bit."

"Well, see if you can get this bloody thing to work."

"What's the problem?"

"It won't fucking work! That's the bloody problem."

"I'll see if I can play with it."

"Good luck." Douglas returns to the kitchen for more coffee.

Left alone for a few minutes, I reformat the printer and it begins clattering away, vibrating the filing cabinet it sits on. Proposal for the Delimitation and Protection of Huaorani Territory comes rattling out. Reading it I begin to get a clearer picture of what RIC is up to.

The proposal outlines an eleven step plan to insure the self-determination of the Huaorani Nation. Part of the plan is the current project, the demarcation of the Huaorani Territory granted in 1990. Because the Huaorani are nomadic, creating a physical boundary is necessary to keep the colonists and *petroleros* out. This five meter line cut with machetes would be planted with distinguishable native species such as *mani de arbol* and *chontaduro*, and posted with warning signs. In this manner the Huaorani would have legal recourse in preventing the shrinkage of their territory. The line was begun by COFENIAE (the Confederation of Indigenous Nations of the Ecuadorian Amazon), but didn't involve the Huaorani. Working in cooperation with the Huaorani (as RIC intends) would serve to make it their own.

With the printer clicking away, Douglas becomes enthusiastic about my participation in the Huaorani project. And more accepting when I casually mention that my former roommate is currently serving a jail term in Malaysia for leading a logging blockade with RIC-Australia. Protesting the destructive logging of the Sarawak Rainforest, home of the Penan (like the Huaorani one of the last nomadic rainforest peoples), they climbed aboard a freighter carrying Sarawak logs to Japan. The Malay government didn't take kindly to this civil disobedience and charged them with trespassing and sentenced each of the protesters to several months in prison.

The action received heavy press coverage in Europe, Asia, and Australia.

With the backing of COFENIAE and IERAC (the Ecuadorian government's Department of Interior), the Huaorani project seems perfectly legal and straightforward. I have no intention of languishing in an Ecuadorian jail.

Douglas invites me to help with the continuing Huaorani project, joining Sparrow, Kevin, and Ali, an Iranian from Santa Fe, New Mexico. We would be in the rainforest for four weeks, living and working with the Huaorani, hacking line through the jungle and teaching the Huaorani about outboard motors.

In a gracious move at pacifying the Huaorani, Petroecuador will be presenting them with a number of outboard motors next month. Douglas lobbied Petroecuador to allow RIC to conduct an extensive workshop on how to use and maintain the motors after the presentation. The Huaorani live in a nonlinear world, and we're going to teach them about outboard motors?

Sparrow thinks that with the increased mobility motors provide, the Huaorani can better communicate and become politically organized. Douglas also emphasizes that the Huaorani could disperse the harvest of the chambira palm used in making chrigra bags for export, thus creating a sustainable economy. Motors and cash for making chrigra bags, then what happens? Money and gas; is that what the Huaorani need?

I admit it's not a matter of preserving a quaint culture as a museum piece, but of allowing a people's basic right to self-determination, and I certainly don't feel comfortable suggesting someone continue living in the Stone Age because I think it's nifty. I suppose there's no such thing as cultural purity. People borrow what they need from other cultures and discard what doesn't work. Demanding purity may just be another form of colonialism. On the other hand, I wonder about creating a dependence upon petroleum, then saying "Sorry, all out."

The Sioux Indians speak of the sixth generation when making decisions; the elders ask themselves, "How will this effect the sixth generation." Imagine thinking of your great-great-great-great-grandchildren when making a decision. What will the world be like for the sixth generation?

The world is closing in on the Huaorani. It seems they only have one option. The oil companies and government will drive them to extinction unless they change; by laying down their spears and stopping attacks on one another, by learning Spanish, and by instituting a political system and demanding rights and recognition.

The legacy of colonialism reaches out from the past and plunges headfirst into the future like a fugue rising and falling with varied specifics but with the same theme. Compare the indifference of the Spanish toward the Andean Indians, except as impediments or slave labor, in their quest for material riches, to the petroleum companies' exploitation of the rainforest. We've learned a few things in the past 500 years, namely that it's cheaper in the long run to give the natives what they ask for, clothes, machetes, and food in trade for destroying them. Perhaps even more diabolical, at least in the eyes of highly spiritual indigenous people, was, and is, the attempts of missionaries, Catholic and now evangelical, robbing them of their souls. Substitute the zealous Franciscan monks following the Spanish for the Summer Institute of Linguistics.

And what about the CIA, the Peace Corps, World Bank Development projects, North American TV shows, clothes, music, technology, and values? At what point does colonization cease? Although monetary gain is a huge part of this, the opening of new markets, the expand and grow philosophy, a deeper motivation may lie under GI JOE, evangelism, and free trade.

It is not just the quest for natural resources or labor that drives the machine of conquest; perhaps the missionaries are close to the truth. We must convert the heathens to the dominant paradigm, for we cannot bear to recognize that there may be another path for humanity. The notion that progress moves forward through time, that the GNP will keep growing is the only justification for our society's existence. If a group of people can thrive completely independent of that notion, they are living proof that the notion must be faulty. "Primitive tribes" are discovered and documented and can then become living specimens. Once we've encapsulated them in the Handbook of South American Indians, we own them. We have their name. People living in a different manner, separate and unknown, threatens and frightens us as much as it intrigues us. And so it is with wildness. We fear wildness, and thus feel compelled to tame it, measure it, map it, quantify it and imprison it.

I just hope Sparrow's right, the Huaorani will be the Huaorani with or without outboard motors.

Hacienda on the Rio Guayllambamba

Perhaps what we really fear from the exploding populations of the world is that they will challenge the superiority of our own subgroup and compromise our survival as the biggest, richest, greediest and most numerous group on earth.
—Germaine Greer

Logging, mining, and other industrial activities do not result from population pressure. —Catherine Caufield

Hanging out at RIC, I begin to learn something of the various projects they are involved with. Besides the Huaorani demarcation project, RIC is working to protect a sacred mountain and beginning a permaculture project in the Andes. Marta, a Colombian, works on sustainable forestry on the coast. Sparrow is involved with an ethnobotany project in conjunction with the University of Missouri, and RIC is establishing a biological reserve at the southern end of Cotacachi National Park with the help of José, a fast talking expatriate hippie.

Just past forty years old, Jose has lived outside the United States for over twenty years. He worked on haciendas and palm oil plantations, owned a bar in the Dominican Republic and is now settling down in Ecuador, although Jose gives the impression of anything but settled. He talks so fast, fingering his *Lagrimas de San Pedro* necklace, pulling his frazzled black hair out of his face, and waving a cigarette around to illustrate his point, that my ears can hardly keep up.

Los Cedros, the biological reserve in the cloud forest, lies at the southern end of the great Choco ecosystem, one of the most unknown and unstudied ecosystems on Earth. Although they share many of the same species, the cloud forest of the Pacific slope of the Andes, unlike the rainforest in the Amazon basin, has distinct wet and dry seasons. Luckily the wet season is just ending. Jose invites me to return with him to Los Cedros where he lives, to help cut trails for the UCLA biologists arriving next week to conduct mammal studies. Since we would not be leaving for the Huaorani Territory for a couple weeks, I decide to join him.

Jose and I fight for a seat on the seven a.m. bus from Quito. Only three times a week does the bus travel to Sanjuangal, the small village from where we have an all day hike to Los Cedros. Anticipating the crowd, Jose bought tickets the day before, reserving seats. Still, I feel bad about kicking out the woman sitting in our seats. Jose handles it with Ecuadorian tact, waving the ticket in front of her face and repeatedly insisting she move. Reluctantly she gathers her bulk and hefts herself out. By now the bus is so crowded we have to climb up on the seat and over. As the bus lurches off, the woman looms over me half sitting, wedged in place by the people still climbing aboard. Cigarette smoke and body heat contribute my advancing claustrophobia, and by the time we reach the village of Nano an hour later, I'm sure I can't take another eight hours of this. So I climb out the window and scamper on top of the bus. Fashioning a seat out of sugar sacks lashed to the roof, I enjoy an open air bus ride through the countryside, soaking up the morning sun and watching the clouds.

The bus wheezes up a narrow cobblestone road. Past Nano the road turns to dirt and we leave the pastures and fincas behind. The road winds down the mountains and into a steep canyon, which squeezes the bus on both sides with thick forest. I have to lie down to keep from getting whacked by overhanging branches.

A mud slide blocks the road. Everyone climbs off and a group of us set to work leveling the mud, while others stretch their legs. A few kids run down to play in the river. Everyone seems to know the bus won't be moving anytime soon.

Jose joins some of the men kicking rocks out of the road. I grab a branch and loosen dirt along the steep bank while others scoop up the pudding-like mud by hand. A couple of shovels would be handy right about now. *There you go again, being the gringo with all the answers.*

On the far side of the road, another group pushes mud down into the river. Their efforts cause chunks of road to collapse into the river as well. The driver and a couple men change the tire on the left side to a larger one to get more clearance leaving the left side of the bus several inches higher than the right. I can't imagine that this will affect the ride.

A dozen people can move a lot of dirt in a short time, almost as much as one person with a shovel, and after three tries, the bus sloshes through the mud and scree and we reload. As we peak out of the canyon, fincas and small towns appear along the rolling hills.

The dusty town plazas merge, Santo Domingo, Ottochacchi, Payacalle. Several hours pass before we descend into a cloud shrouded valley. By now, the road has degenerated to little more than a dirt two-track leading to Sanjuangal, the end of the line. The twenty people left retrieve their gear from the roof and disappear into this town of maybe a dozen buildings. This town and the road to it aren't even on the map. Quito is the nearest city, eight hours by bus. However, Otavalo is only forty kilometers away— by trail.

Jose and I head to the hotel/restaurant, a deluxe cinder block and wood shack run by the alcalde. Thin planks separate the rooms upstairs. The local "dentist" pulls a small girl's tooth out in one room, and in the other sit two tables and a propane camp stove. There is no electricity or plumbing or even outhouses in Sanjuangal. I should never have complained about the lack of toilet seats.

The alcalde cheerily greets us and gives us a couple beers. The rain turns the town into a muddy Márquez novel. The "inn" is low on food, but the alcalde's wife manages to cook us each a meal of rice and beans, fried egg and a piece of chicken. After the meal Jose pays, adding his bill from the previous visit—four beers, three meals and one night lodging comes to a grand total of four dollars.

After eating, we walk the two miles to Don Pepe's hacienda in the rain. After the long, dusty bus ride and the muddy hike, I begin looking forward to a hot shower and a bed at the hacienda.

As we walk, we stop and shake hands with everyone we see. In what is apparently a highly regarded social ritual, even in the pouring rain, everyone says, "*buenas tardes*" and shakes hands with everyone else. Jose carries on an abbreviated conversation, "*Sí, sí, Quito, bien, sí.*" Then everyone says "*luego*" and shakes hands with everyone else again.

At Don Pepe's, half a dozen people watch a soggy Ecuabally game.

Ecuabally, the Ecuadorian version of volleyball, is played with just three players and a higher net. A player is allowed to hold the ball in his outstretched palms for a few seconds, almost like a free shot in basketball.

I grimace. *We can't shake everyone's hand.*

Thankfully, Jose hurries by the crowd repeating, *"Buenas tardes, buenas tardes."* This custom of acknowledging everyone's existence is pleasant, but trying.

Jose unlocks his room on the ground floor.

"It smells like rat piss," He looks at me. "But that's the way it is."

I look through the musty darkness. A saddle sits crammed in one corner next to a plank bed with a disgusting mattress and a dirty blanket.

"I guess we'll find somewhere for you to sleep," he says.

Thank God.

Twenty years ago Don Pepe, son of Czechoslovakian immigrants, carved this hacienda out of the forest. Across the Rio Guayllambamba, a raging muddy torrent, cloud forest still blankets the hillside.

The "hacienda" turns out to be a two story open wooden structure, not quite what I expected. Instead of windows, half walls let in the air and sunshine while pillars support the roof. The back opens to the cloud forest, the front to the Ecuabally court, chickens and dogs. A tiled kitchen opens to a grapefruit tree, and a pulley system lowers kitchen scraps to the ground. On the wooden kitchen wall hangs a Czechoslovakian serving platter with a silver rim and a portrayal of 18th century upper class Europeans playing piano, flute and violin in a sitting room, like a scene from Amadeus. Below hangs a Nippon portable radio on a nail. Next to it is thumbtacked a calendar from a hardware store in Quito. Kerosene lamps hang from the ceiling, and pineapples sit in a basket under a Virgin Mary clock.

People constantly come and go in the house. A boy brings a load of firewood and corncobs for the Doña's stove. Two little girls cart in a sack of yuca. Dogs wander in and the Doña chases them out with a broom, while the cat sneaks along the windowsill trying to steal a scrap. The Doña, a tired, old woman who stares at the campo and mutters to herself, pounds yuca with a rock.

Gracilla, the twenty-four year old daughter, updates Jose on the local gossip, while we dry off and chew panella, raw brown sugar pulled like taffy.

In the nearby shed an ancient tractor lies in pieces. The threads of these bolts haven't seen fresh oil in fifty years. Don Pepe, up to his arms in grime, pokes at a motor, a smile on his weathered Czech face. Don Pepe sporting a crop of thick white hair, wears a cap his wife knitted and boasts a crumpled, grumpy, but benevolent face. He must be sixty or seventy years old; I can't really tell.

Jorge, the son, a strong blond boy, likes working on the tractors. He proudly shows me a thick book which translates American automotive terms to Spanish so he can order parts from the United States. I see the problem; I would have no idea how to find the Spanish word for "sparkplug" much less "crankshaft thrust bearing." Sitting at the kitchen table, Gracilla shows me Jorge's wedding pictures. He just got married to the local school teacher. No one looked happy.

Three girls play barefoot on a minibike in front of the house. The wildhair oldest, maybe eight, holds a baby. The other, about four, trips and falls on her dirt smudged face. Wildhair holds out her free hand to help. Something clicks inside, and I glimpse something nameless, which seems so obvious on the campo and so hidden in my everyday existence.

For dinner Gracilla serves soup made with huge arrowhead shaped leaves of the *papacuno*, the bread and sausages Jose brought, and pineapple for dessert. We eat off old plates from Czechoslovakia.

Doña and Gracilla eat in the kitchen after the men are served. Coffee grown and ground on the hacienda follows dinner. All the food Don Pepe's family eats is grown or raised on the hacienda, except white sugar, salt, cooking oil, wheat flour, and tuna fish. Don Pepe draws on the table with thick stumpy fingers and scrunches up his face, peering at you with bright blue eyes making his big Czech chin stick out.

While Don Pepe devours the newspaper Jose brought from Quito, a *campesino* family comes by with the friends and relations of a little boy who has an earache. Don Pepe comes out of his reading revelry and administers medicine to the boy. Suddenly I am in Africa with the great white land-owner helping the poor landworker. Or on a southern plantation. All the *campesinos* defer to Don Pepe. How can someone come in here with nothing, bust his ass for years, and have dozens of campesinos living in shacks working his land? Is it because he's white—an entitlement assumed and propagated by both white and nonwhite?

The white ten to fifteen percent of the population controls most of Ecuador's resources and exclusively dominates the upper classes. Indians, who comprise half of the population, own the poorest parcels of land or work on haciendas. Most do not speak Spanish, and rarely live beyond a subsistence economy. Mestizos, stuck somewhere in the middle, occasionally break into the merchant class, but most work in the fields.

During the colonial period, the King of Spain granted most of the fertile lands to the conquistadors who became *encomiendaros*, extracting a tribute of cash, blankets, corn and chickens from the Indians whose land it had once been. Much of the mestizo population resulted from young women being taken for tribute.

In return the *encomiendaro* was to instruct the natives in the Catholic faith. The priests also extracted tribute in addition to their wages from the *encomiendaro*. Since they were not permitted by law to live on their *encomiendaro*, *encomiendaros* used the Inca hierarchy of *curacas* or local chiefs. In many cases the native *curacas* were more cruel and tyrannical than their Spanish overlords, keeping a portion of the toll for themselves. However, many of the *curacas* who tried to stick up for the Indians found themselves tortured, burned, or imprisoned.

Many of the natives were literally worked to death by the Spanish. Several observers called it worse than slavery. One sixteenth century Spanish chronicler noted, "In 18 years half the natives have expired in many *repartimientos* on the coastal plain, because of the excessive work given to them by their *ecomienderos*."

Thousands more died as porters as the conquistadors took "Indians in chains to carry what they had pillaged… when Indians grew exhausted, they cut off their heads without untying them from the chains, leaving the roads full of dead bodies."

"The mass of Peruvians, the *hatunruna*, of the Inca empire, saw an Inca master replaced by a Spaniard; but they lost heavily on the exchange," reports John Hemming in *The Conquest of the Incas*.

And only four hundred years later, the 1964 Agrarian Reform Act outlawed tenant farming. Under this system the tenant worked for the hacienda several days a week in return for a house site and a small plot of land (usually the most unproductive). A number of Indians have become small landowners since then, eking out a living on plots high on the hillsides, nine out of ten of which are too small or too marginal to support a family. And half of them are still landless. In all of Latin America, seven percent of landowners own ninety-three percent of the arable land.

Jose says because Don Pepe has tractors and can plant a lot of crops, the *campesinos* are better off working for him; they make more money and have less work and worries.

His fly broken halfway open, a man loads grapefruit into a cardboard box outside my door. The roosters are quiet now after crowing at four a.m.

For breakfast we eat fried plantains with loads of good strong coffee.

After Don Pepe, Jorge, and Jose leave, Gracilla cooks up a ripe plantain for me to try, it's much sweeter.

An old woman brings by a couple of *platanos* baked in mani (peanut) sauce as a gift. Looking closer at the wrinkled face, I realize the "old woman" must be in her forties.

The women are always working. Gracilla never stops moving from feeding the chickens, to weeding the garden, to cooking for Pepe, and cleaning the house. She tells me she went to high school in Quito and worked there for two years but didn't like it.

"Hay mucho trabajo, hasta la sies de la mañana hasta las nueve de la noche. Cada dia. Me gusta el campo," Gracilla says and means it. "There's a lot of work, from six in the morning to nine at night. Every day. But I like the ranch."

Gracilla shows me her garden, with *papacuno*, avocado and papaya trees, aji bushes, kale. A turkey struts bold red flaps of skin around the yard. I ask about a tree with long, drooping fruit like zucchini. She tells me it's luffa. Gracilla pulls one off the tree. Taking it to an outdoor sink, she smashes it with her hands. As she kneads the fruit against the counter, the thick green skin peels off, revealing white fibrous insides. Washing and twisting, Gracilla squeezes the seeds and pulp out of the spongy mass. She hangs it on the clothes line to dry, and says that I can take it with me to use when bathing to scrape off the dead skin. Gracilla then shows me the rows of luffa drying in a hut. She says they sell them in Quito. I always thought luffa was a sponge or some sort of underwater creature. I never imagined it grew on trees.

So many things grow here, so many forms of life everywhere. It's so green and growing and fruitful that it's frightening. It stinks of life. I need a little starkness, a little death.

A man stands on the wooden suspension bridge throwing grain into the grey morning. The breeze blows the chaff into the roaring chocolate river below.

A couple of neighbors are invited for lunch. We have plantain and barley soup, yet another variety of plantain, and yuca topped with *papacuno* sauce, rice and tuna fish, cane juice, and of course, coffee.

I go with Jose to catch his horse, a small grey gelding Paseo named Sandoz. In his usual fastball manner, Jose explains the paseo gait and the breed, "It's smooth, man, from Columbia, starting to catch on in the States, but down here, they all use it, smooth run so they can carry a drink without spilling it. Give it a try."

A rope looped through Sandoz's mouth functions as a bit and reins. I hop on and trot off, breaking him into a paseo easily. As he begins to run, I nearly slip off, not having done much bareback riding. When I return, still intact, Jose saddles him for the trip to town. Jose throws a couple grain sacks on Sandoz as a saddle blanket, then straps on an old army mule saddle—two pieces of wood collared with leather. Two pieces of wood and a fanbelt serve as a stirrup. Jose tightens a rope cinch and a rope under Sandoz's tail. Sandoz exhibits several open sores on his back from the saddle.

For dinner Gracilla serves hot breadfruit, cooked for two hours so the shells are soft and peel right off. Breadfruit tastes like, well, bread and fruit... and a little nutty. We also eat soup and bread baked with yuca flour and filled with squash jelly.

After dinner a campesino family drops in. The young mother has malaria and the baby is malnourished. Gracilla treats them as best she can, giving the mother a malaria shot and some goat's milk for the baby. After they leave, Gracilla sits down with a cup of strong coffee. She says that so many people have children at a young age. One girl had five abortions—or rather aborted five times—by the time she was fifteen. Another girl had a child at twelve.

"How old was the father?" I ask. Gracilla says that the baby's father is the girl's stepfather.

Others have five to eight kids—all starving, or at least malnourished.

Jose points at his head and says in Spanglish, "*Es la capicidad intellectual. Los niños no toman leche y protein.* So they don't develop. All the people eat is *arroz blanco, yuca y pan blanco y Coke.*"

"*Es la educacion, no?*" I ask.

"*Claro,*" says Gracilla.

"Can't they teach the kids nutrition and sex ed?" I ask.

"The teachers are bad. They can't even teach the kids how to shit. *Son tontos.* It doesn't take education to figure out that if your five kids aren't getting enough to eat, adding more kids makes it worse," says Jose.

Numerous United Nations studies link malnutrition with irreparable brain damage twisting the spiral of poverty even tighter. Neo-natal care is non-existent; the best most can hope for is enough food when the baby is born. How do you persuade parents of the importance of family planing and long term strategies when they often don't know where their next meal is coming from?

An appalling educational system, a corrupt government, environmental destruction, rampant sexual abuse, mass poverty, overpopulation, a poor diet of starch and sugar in a land bulging with food, a staggering debt and no revolution in sight. Where do you start? In many ways the Third World is ahead of us. The United States is on the way to entering the spiral, if it hasn't already, especially in the inner cities.

The reaction of many populations to stressful environmental conditions is to have more offspring. When conditions are favorable, survival rates are high, necessitating few offspring. When environmental conditions deteriorate, more young are produced so as to increase the chances of survival.

If we can presume to extrapolate to human biology (a dangerous proposition, but somebody's got to do it), adverse environmental conditions whether it be pollution, famine, warfare, disease, poverty, or exploitation, may serve as a stimulus for population GROWTH.

Overpopulation can also be traced upward to the international debt crisis. In order to make payments on massive loans, Third World countries cut social welfare programs and put land into export production. Not only does this force people off the land, but they no longer grow food for consumption. Instead they have to buy food (mostly white rice and sugar), thus increasing poverty and malnutrition at the same time. The newly instituted free trade agreements will only exacerbate the situation by providing food cheaper than the campesinos can grow it. Canadian corn and U.S. rice will drive the remaining landholders into the cities or into growing export crops dependent upon the whims of the world market.

A loss of land results in a loss of security, which is compensated for by having more children: to provide for parents in old age, as a work force, and to insure their survival in the face of high infant mortality.

Unequal power structures and land ownership patterns come to a head in family relations. Denied meaningful work, men cling to the only power they retain, that over women. The low self-respect which comes from being unable to support a family can lead men to move in and out of relationships.

Gracilla blames machismo. *"Tengo una factoria nueva,"* a man says to describe his new bride. "I have a new factory."

Community attitudes, as well as machismo, pressure women to keep having children until bearing a son, further stressing an already malnourished family. This powerlessness results in perpetual motherhood. If women were given a choice, how many children would they have?

A study of women in Quito and Guayaquil consistently linked low social-economic status and high fertility. For example, women with a high school education averaged fewer than two children, while women with no formal education had more than five children. For many women fertility may be their only choice.

This study was done in 1965! What's going on here? Somebody's not listening. We've known this for nearly thirty years and haven't done a thing. The wolf pack and the condom are both behavioral adaptations to limiting population growth. Social changes, as well as improving environmental conditions, are the only effective long term solutions to overpopulation. Not only do people need clean air and water, but also a healthy state of being, enough to eat, right livelihood, access to education and liberation of women.

A few Third World countries (Cuba, Colombia, Burma, Sri Lanka), have reduced their population growth to less than two percent. Access to a basic diet, expenditures on public health, and increased female literacy are considered the primary factors. Social changes that empower people reduce population growth, according to Frances Moore Lappé and Rachel Schurman.

They write, "High birth rates among the poor can best be understood as a defensive response against structures of power that fail to provide—or actively block access to—a source of security beyond the family."

"The point is simply that when we see the hopelessness of the slums and barrios, we see the latest stages of an epidemic disease that has become endemic in it's later stages. It was the scourge of colonialism that cheapened human life, that made human dignity a nonsense, that showed the people in the hot lands that their dignity was not theirs to command. As long as the situation continues, as long as they have no resource base of their own, as long as they are mocked by the demands of foreign economies, they will have no reason to wish to be fewer," states Germaine Greer.

However, not everyone needs to become like the developed world. In fact, one rich, white kid in the United States uses ten times the resources as a child in Brazil. Wendell Berry states that even one person with the access and will to use atomic weapons is too many, illustrating that it's not purely the numbers of people that should concern us so much as what those people are <u>doing.</u>

Overpopulation is often blamed as the culprit for tropical deforestation, usually with the implication that the tropical countries are overpopulated. However, inequitable land distribution is the underlying cause.

"Among the rainforest countries, only Haiti, India, and the Philippines have a population density higher than 400 people per square mile; Italy, Japan, Great Britain, Belgium, the Netherlands, and West Germany all have more than 500. . . . Taking potential farmland into account but still leaving aside Amazonia, each person in Brazil could have 10 acres. Instead, 4.5 percent of Brazil's landowners own 81 percent of the country's farmland, and 70 percent of rural households are landless," writes Catherine Caufield.

Perhaps it's the Northern countries which are overpopulated, however it is not as evident because we extract our needs and resources from the tropics, forcing the people there into marginal existence. In order to keep our house clean and tidy, we've stuffed all our junk into the Third World closet and shut the door.

THE GOLDEN QUETZAL

The human body evolved on this planet in close contact with the earth. Breaking these bonds with the earth leads to peculiar types of insanities found in cities. Breaking the bonds with the earth causes the "paper realities" of civilization to encroach upon one's consciousness to a point where one believes that the paper reality is real, rather than a convenient construction of man. —John Lilly.

A beautiful morning dawns sunny and hot with blue skies, green forest, and a chocolate river. A miserable day for hiking. I'm dripping sweat as soon as we cross the bridge over the Rio Guayllambamba and begin hiking up the trail. The red and black clay saturated by the rains, turns the trail into thick, slippery goo. I walk behind the horse, Sandoz, who, loaded with supplies, keeps slipping and stumbling through the muck. The mud sucks my boots down into the earth. Solid ground must be down there somewhere. As I take a step, my foot comes halfway out of the boot before the mud unwillingly releases it with a hollow slurping sound.

"This is the bad section, hey?" says Jose, glancing back. "The trail to Otavalo is like this the whole way and then there's the bad parts," Jose laughs and slurps on ahead.

After a couple of hot hours Jose announces, "Maria Ellena's is just right up here a bit. We can get a couple beers."

BEER! Oh, this is too good to be true. Beer!! I'm hot and sweaty and about to sit in the shade and drink a beer. Hahahahah beerbeer beerbeerbeer. At the top of the hill sits a wooden house. Jose ties Sandoz to a post and we walk over to the woman washing clothes.

"*Dos cervezas,*" says Jose.

"*No hay,*" says the woman not looking up.

"*No hay! Si, claro hay.*"

"*No hay,*" she repeats.

All she has is warm Coke. We are both rather disappointed. We drink warm Coke, eat sardines and crackers and think about cold beer.

Maria Ellena mentions that someone's working Hector's land.

"Who? Who? *Quien esta?*" asks Jose excitedly.

"*No se. Mala gente,*" she says. "Bad people."

A cluster of small houses squats across the river from Maria Ellena's. Jose points out a long, prefab metal building. "That's the *evangelica* church. The Catholics have been in these little villages for years and the *evangelicos* come in, give them food and shovels and convert everybody. It drives the priests nuts, hey?"

"There's two churches here?"

"Sure. That white building is the Catholic church."

"How many people . . ."

"A couple dozen. It's crazy, hey?"

From Maria Ellena's the trail rises steeply above the river. At a turn in the trail squats a big rock. Carved about the rock are dozens of spiral petroglyphs left by an ancient forest culture. Lichen covered and worn smooth, they've been here hundreds if not thousands of years.

"I figure it's a boundary marker. Different group of people up here telling the folks below to keep out," says Jose.

Hot and sweaty and lost in thought, I trudge through the muck. Suddenly on my left, a machete rises a few inches from my face. Jumping from fright, I nearly fall backwards. Off the trail, stands a small man with a large machete. He breaks out laughing. I grab his shoulder for support and to make sure he is really there. He appeared so suddenly. Or rather, he was standing there the whole time, quiet, politely waiting for us to pass, and I failed to notice until I was nearly on top of him.

After a long, hot, muddy eight hour hike up the Los Cedros River, we arrive at a tired wooden house. We walk through the yard of chickens to the watering trough. After drinking from the trough, I splash water over my grimy head. *Just like being in the Old West.* A woman comes over, and Jose buys some cheese wrapped in banana leaves. She also thinks men may be working Hector's land, but she doesn't know.

A few minutes later we descend the hill to Jose's place, more of a field camp than anything else. Plastic tarps keep the rain off the open air shacks. Jose's partner, Juan, is jonesing for some Triago, a cheap cane alcohol.

"Only brought one bottle, Juan, you know what it does to you. Now we're not going to drink it all at once," says Jose.

Gracilla had hinted that both Juan and Jose are "recovering" alcoholics.

Behind the shacks lies an old garden and banana patch. Yellow-rumped tanagers with deep black backs, vibrant yellow rumps and bright blue beaks hang upside down among the bananas gleaning insects off the broad leaves. Jose and Juan don't seem concerned with keeping nature at bay and the garden has progressed into a blend of wild and cultivated plants.

A bird lands on a naranjilla leaf. The broad leaves with purple veins, the underside covered with purple hairs, lead to a thick stalk and a fuzzy orange naranjilla. Cut a naranjilla open and you see a green, juicy fruit with hundreds of tiny seeds. It looks and tastes like a sour kiwi fruit. Delicious!

"I've got six different kinds of bananas here," says Jose as we eat the huge platanos covered in mani sauce. "Four of them are cooking bananas. Those over there are the *manzanas*.¬ Taste well, kinda like apples, man. I also got your regular Ecuadorian export bananas that people you know buy by the pound. I can't believe that people buy bananas by the fucking pound, man. Here I give them to the wild animals." In fact, Juan just saw a brown agouti munching on some bananas below camp at dusk.

Relatives of guinea pigs and the paca, agoutis are a fairly common large rodent. Sort of like a giant squirrel, agoutis bury seeds for later retrieval, while the larger paca stores fat which gives it the body of a small pig behind a narrow squirrel face.

To harvest the bananas, Jose cuts down the tree. I guess its more like a big stalk, with three, maybe four, whacks with a machete. The banana blood oozes out the gaping wound. It looks delicious.

"Don't get that junk on your clothes. It'll never come off," warns Juan when I stick my finger under the dripping sap.

A green bunch of bananas crashes to the ground. They will turn yellow and ripen in a couple days. Birds and fruit bats have eaten all the ripe ones still on the trees. We leave some on the ground for the agoutis and weasels.

Bananas, originally from India, Burma, and the Philippines were first introduced to the New World in 1516. Because they are hybrids, commercial bananas cannot pollinate themselves and must be artificially pollinated.

The Los Cedros River splashes clear with a green-blue tint through boulders and deep pools. Vines dangle above the pool. Moss blankets the rocks, and epiphytes cloak the trees. Surfboard-sized leaves sprout out of a thick stalk and hang over the river. Such incredible diversity of shapes and shades of green.

It's obvious people are tropical animals, I think, crouched on a rock, naked and dripping wet from jumping into a jungle pool. I look at my body. There's no fur. I wouldn't last long like this outside of the tropics. Way, way back the rainforest is our home. Is this sense of homecoming part of our fascination with the rainforest? Humans inhabit a landscape. How does landscape affect our behavior, our language, our thoughts, our soul?

Large, tree-dwelling snakes often prey on monkeys, their only natural enemy in the Old World. Jung said that human's paranoid fear of snakes is part of our collective unconscious from when we lived in trees--not so long ago really. That feeling you get just before falling asleep, when your body jerks like you're grabbing on to something, also stems from living in trees. The only other danger a monkey faces is falling out of the canopy when asleep.

Humans live in the rainforest unencumbered; the forest provides for everything. It would be impossible to die from starvation with all this food lying around, fruit and nuts and leaves and roots. And it never gets cold, even at night. No wonder the Huaorani regard death as unnatural.

I look over at all my stuff sitting on the rock. A quick inventory reveals: water bottle, binoculars, (actually Jose's, I dropped mine in the creek yesterday) large green REI daypack with oil stains and busted zipper and hole ripped in the bottom, machete, rubber boots, camera, extra shirt for rain, notebook, bag of peanuts, roll of film, key to the RIC house in Quito, spare batteries, bug juice, pocket knife.

What happens when we become domesticated like the banana, yuca, and leaf cutter ant fungus, all of which cannot survive on their own? Have we fully domesticated ourselves? Is this why our culture fears wildness so much—it reminds us of who we really are, of our origins?

"With a fantastic collection of stamps to win friends and influence his uncle," the Tombstone Blues crackle from Jose's small battery powered tape player. He rocks back and forth cleaning his revolver when I return from the river.

"Protection, man. We don't know who's up there. We just want to buy the land, man, but they might not understand. I'm going to try and talk with them about, you know, saving the land, and not shooting the monkeys, but this Hector, he's killed people and escaped from jail three times. I don't think he's around, but his uncle's up there and he busted Hector out of prison, you just never know, man. We don't know what they're doin' up there or why or how many, or if they even want to see our gringo faces, but I'm just gonna go talk to them, man."

I gradually derive from Jose that RIC, in cooperation with IERAC (the Ecuadorian Department of Interior) is buying land along the Los Cedros River to form a biological reserve which will buffer the 500,000 acre Cotacachi National Park from encroaching colonization. Hector's land is the last piece up the valley. But Hector is long gone. He killed a fellow some years ago, escaped from jail a couple times since, and is still on the loose. Someone working Hector's land means they somehow bought it from him and might not be willing sellers. Furthermore, they are in the process of clearing it for cultivation, and possibly taking potshots at the endangered Brown-headed Spider Monkey.

The following morning, Jose, Juan and I head through a cleared field to where a man is cutting lumber with a chainsaw, slicing the trees lengthwise. He also thinks there may be someone up there but won't say for sure. We hear shouts from below, so we take the trail through the pasture and into the trees where a man, woman, child and cows are standing in the forest stream. They tell us that there are indeed four "*mala gentes*" working Hector's land.

We hike up a ridge through several pastures. At the top of the ridge we drop down through the forest to a branch of the Cedros.

I walk slow, mouth agape at the enveloping forest. A bright red-orange millipede crawls over huge, fallen leaves. I pick him up and he curls in a tight spiral, a black line down his back, a spiral within a spiral in a non-repeating pattern. Jose and Juan are far down the trail. I drop the millipede and hurry on. We cross the river and head up the other side, no longer following a trail, but rather a machete path through the forest.

As we start up the hill we hear a couple shots.

"Now remember, man, let me do all the talking," Jose says.

"No problema," I say.

Suddenly we are standing in a cut. Cecropia trees lie everywhere in a broken jumble. Smoke rises from a hut on the top of the hill. One last cedar tree rises behind the clearing. Beyond in all directions stretches unbroken forest. *These are the guys who freed a murderer from jail and we're in the middle of nowhere and we would never be missed and our bodies would be tossed to rot in the jungle and in two days would be completely decomposed.*

Stumbling over the fallen trees, we "*buenas tardes*" and "*Como les van*" our way up the hill to the open shelter. Four men stand around cooking a pot of lunch on a fire. Machetes are propped up against the shelter and an ancient rusty shotgun lies alongside. Two crested guans, large turkey-like birds, hang by their feet from the crossbeams. *They seem friendly enough. Nothing but Ecuadorian rednecks out destroying the countryside. Nothing to be frightened of.*

Jose gets right to the point. He wants to buy the land for a nature preserve. He explains the need to protect headwaters and monkeys and plants for medicine. They agree that, yes, it is a very nice place and would sell it to Jose, but they have already done much work on it making this nice clearing and shelter and have to be compensated for their labor.

In Ecuador, as in much of Latin America, land itself is worth little. Labor, or "improvements" on land, contain the value. Deforestation equals legal title. At the current rate of deforestation, Ecuador will lose half of its forest in the next ten years.

Jose suspects these guys heard someone was interested in buying it, so they hurried over to do as much work as possible so they could charge more for the property.

"*Hablamos, hablamos ahora. Cuanto quiere,*" Jose is in a buying mood. "Let's talk now. How much to you want?"

"How much did you pay for it? We'll give you what you paid plus your labor."

"It was very cheap because I done a lot of favors for Hector," the older man replies.

"*Hablamos, hablamos,*" Jose repeats.

It's not like RIC has funds available for land purchases or an investment portfolio. Fortunately, last week RIC received a $1000 donation from a woman in Santa Fe to buy land and dedicate a tree in memory of her daughter.

Eventually Jose talked them down to $1000.

"What do you guys think? Is $1000 a fair price?" Jose asks us. "We're getting ripped off, of course."

I shrug. "Do they have any papers?"

"No, but he says he's done Hector a lot of favors and the land's his. He'll sign the papers stating he's the owner to sell the property," Jose says.

"Will they stop cutting and go away," I ask.

"Tomorrow."

So Jose and the man arrange to meet tomorrow to seal the deal for $250 of Sparrow's money Jose has for emergencies. He will receive the rest in Quito when he signs the papers next week. The whole deal takes just over an hour.

I don't think this is quite how the Nature Conservancy operates.

As we pick our way back through the fallen trees, an occasional banana tree in the mist of the second growth cecropia, or *guarumo*, trees indicates that this area was cultivated many years before. These cecropia trees I find so fascinating are not much more than a weed, a short lived (twenty years) pioneer species flourishing where the forest has been disturbed. Cecropias traded long life and chemical defense for rapid growth. Lacking any sort of poison, they developed an interesting relationship with Azteca ants. Azteca ants live in the hollow stems and swarm out over the tree attacking caterpillars, other ants and epiphytes and vines, which could weaken the cecropia. In return, the tree provides a sugary substance at the base of its leaf stalks. Cecropias are also the primary food of the three-toed sloth.

Seeing this resilience of nature and rapid revegetation, I'm not entirely convinced that humans are capable of actually "destroying the planet." Granted we can certainly make it a lot less habitable. "Destroying the planet" and "Saving the Earth" strike me as statements of supreme arrogance implying that humans have the ability (if not the will) to consciously change something as ancient and complex as the Earth. And save it from what? Ourselves? In fact, short of human extinction, benign neglect may be the best thing we can do for the planet--give it a chance to heal.

However, we can protect wild land ,and in this tragic world it may be the only thing left worth saving. After humans either reduce or eliminate themselves, biological reserves will remain from which the remaining species can issue forth and re-inhabit their world. By eliminating wild habitat, not only to we remove ourselves from the sacred, but we make it increasingly difficult for nature to recover from the human experiment. Nobody <u>wants</u> to destroy habitat. It's a side effect of our consumptive life-style, just as poverty is a side effect.

We hurry down to the river and celebrate by eating empanadas Juan made this morning. They're delicious—whole wheat, quinoa flour, barley flour, wheat germ and filled with cheese. We spread tuna fish and hot French mustard over them. Tangerines for desert. As we eat, a young man who was at the meeting hurries by with the rusty shotgun in his hand.

"He's wanted," Jose states between bites.

"By who?" I ask.

"The policia, man. That's why he's in a hurry to get out of here, now that we've seen them."

After a couple of hours of walking along the river, we come to the border of Jose's land. Jose realizes that the piece of land we just crossed is unclaimed, but everyone thinks it belongs to Hector, so buying Hector's effectively sandwiches this parcel, protecting it as well.

Jose whips up a "beer substitute," a concoction of lemon juice, (the "lemons" are orange inside and have crinkly green skin, actually sour tangerines) a couple of naranjillas squeezed through a strainer, water, sugar and a shot of traigo. It tastes mostly like traigo. He sets a cup down in front of me, and the fumes just about knock me over.

Juan and Jose take turns cooking very good meals, quite amazing for an open fire. There doesn't seem to be any hassles except when Jose explains how to light a fire.

"You got to have oxygen here, Juan. That's why it's not burning. A fire needs oxygen. That's what makes a fire--oxygen, fuel and heat. You gotta have all three, Juan."

The area around camp certainly <u>looks</u> to have those flat places where Jose said the indigenous people had built houses. It is a strange topography. I ask Jose how you can tell where they are.

"There all around; we're on one now. There's burial mounds all around here. There's one over there." He points with the machete he's using to chop onions. "There's one on the way to the outhouse, hey? The trail takes a sharp turn around it. I try not to step on it. It's a burial mound, man." He raises an eyebrow. Like usual, he hasn't answered my question. Or else he thinks I'm an idiot for not asking exactly the <u>right</u> question, the one he knows the answer to.

It's time once again for BBC Worldwide News. Jose's scratchy radio can barely pick it up, but he has it on constantly. I'm extremely well informed here in the middle of nowhere. Jose sits up close listening intently. Sifting through the static, I catch a line from an interview with Paul Ehrlich warning of the coming environmental catastrophe. "Within twenty to thirty years everyone on the planet will know we've made a huge mistake."

Jose seals the land deal with a down payment of $250 in the banana patch. At eight in the morning, under partly sunny skies, the involved parties sit on a rotting moss covered log to sign the receipts. The clouds lift, revealing mountains draped in trees that have been sealed off from colonization and will be preserved in their natural state. Everyone leaves happy with the deal.

This afternoon I strap on a machete and put on rubber boots. *Jungle Greg going off to hack his way through the wild tropical jungle.* I'm right on the edge of unexplored, uninhabited wild land. *There's jaguars out there!*

But I've got my machete. I'm smack in the middle of a cloud. I have no idea where I really am. Not being able to look at a map and say "This is where I'm standing" is rather unnerving.

Jose, Juan and I hew our way to the top of the ridge, meeting a trail. As we walk, we widen the trail. Gradually we hack less and less, and soon we're walking silently through the knee deep ferns and ducking under vines instead of hacking through, listening to the birds and not wishing to make any noise. In a flash of black and yellow, a pair of oropendolas squawk through the trees and a large, dark shape crashes through the brush.

"A tayra," Juan announces.

"A what?"

"A tayra, I don't know, like a big mink or otter."

Off amongst the foliage sits a large, bright red bird. Binoculars reveal a bright orange crest. A cock-of-the-rock. I don't know many South American birds, but this one is as distinctive as it is rare.

Like sage grouse, the cock-of-the-rock is one of the few birds that breeds in leks, a male display ground where females shop for prospective mates. Numerous males compete with lavish displays on their individual piece of turf for the highly selective hens. After mating, the hen must build a nest, incubate, and raise the young by herself.

I'm still amazed at the lack of bothersome bugs. I keep expecting to be swatting at mosquitoes or cussing black flies or find my back covered by army ants. No insect pests, no snakes drooping from trees.

As we follow the ridge, instead of craning my neck straight up, I look out onto the platforms of mosses and epiphytes suspended in the saddles of the great trees. I begin to recognize certain plants. I can't name them, but notice their large leaf patterns that I've seen before, and the forest no longer seems so foreign, and hence, not so frightening.

One of the most striking things about so many tropical tree species is the prevalence of buttresses supporting the trunks. No one is sure of the purpose of the buttresses. Ecologists think buttresses allow the roots to cover more surface area, enabling the tree to absorb minerals from the nutrient poor soil. John Kichner tells of a team of botanists who were discussing various theories for the purpose of buttresses. Their Indian guide stated that the buttresses were simply to hold up the tree. They quickly dismissed his input. He pulled out his machete and hacked away each of the buttresses of a small tree. He then pushed the tree over.

Another explanation is that buttresses prevent lianas, but again I see many buttressed trees plagued with lianas. Lianas can weigh a tree down so much they break off branches and even cause the collapse of the tree. Some lianas known as strangler figs can encircle a tree and kill it.

The strangler fig or *Matapalo* (tree killer) is a member of the Genus *Ficus* along with 900 other species, which all bear figs. While most lianas start as shrubs, then send out tendrils looping and climbing up the trees, strangler figs begin as a seed dropped by a bird or monkey into a bromeliad and grow downward. The various tentacles of the lianas twist together and support each other. Eventually the strangler fig smothers the host tree. Sealed off, the host tree dies and decomposes, supplying nutrients for its conqueror. The matapalo now stands as a tree on its own with a hollow center where the host tree once stood.

We soon come upon the giant matapalo. "The mother of all matapalos" Jose calls it. This particular matapalo is a huge tree in its own right. Three large trunks merge together at the base. Deep recesses lie hidden within the contorted trunk of lianas. Bending down and looking into the tree, I see a small stream of light coming from the other side. I sit back in the buttressed arms of the great tree while Jose and Juan return to camp. I stare up at the hanging greenery trying to spot birds or monkeys. But I'm not trying very hard, just sitting and listening.

Returning to camp, I stop at a rotten moss covered stump. Numerous plants, epiphytes and ferns, but also woody plants, sprout forth. I count seventeen types of plants that I can easily distinguish. I'm not a botanist, so there are undoubtedly more species. I start keeping an eye out for stumps and soon come across one that is a pillar of moss. It is difficult to tell where stump ends and ground and plants begin. I don't even try counting the species on this one.

I can see and hear rain falling, but none reaches me on the ground; a few drops and a pleasant mist is all. The temperature is constant. Everywhere is life. The earth is so nurturing. It's easy to see why people wouldn't want to give the forest up. What is surprising is that they'll cut it down to make room for cows.

The clouds sink at dusk over the forest, and a fine mist covers everything.

It's now definitely summer—the dry season in the cloud forest when it only rains part of the day. The mornings are nice with patches of blue sky, so I depart for a hike by myself seeking a haven from the static of the BBC Worldwide and Jose's tirades.

BBC's broadcasting "Scott of the Antarctic." In today's episode, Scott has 800 miles to return after finding out Amundsen had gotten to the South

Pole first.

I wander up a side stream of the Cedros, and hack my way around a big
boulder sitting in the middle of the stream. I poke along looking up at the
trees; it's drizzling again but nothing reaches the ground. Around a bend, a
waterfall and a steep granite cliff block the way.

What is it about water, about waterfalls, that draws me so? Is it because it's the only open place in the claustrophobic jungle? I'm having a
little trouble with all the biology going on around me. Tiny white-vented
euphonias, small tanagers which nest in bromeliads, dart about the tall trees.
The root of a liana punches straight through a shelf fungus on its way to the
forest floor. Roots, rocks and leaves look like they're moving. Everything
teems and pulses with life. Plants look like animals and animals look like
plants. I watch an insect that looks like a piece of dried grass lying perfectly still. The only giveaway is its legs which stand out against the forest
floor. It takes close observation to tell which end is which. I poke at it and
it doesn't move. Maybe it really is a twig, I think. So I turn it over and the
legs move a little. Things are not always as they appear. Other insects
resemble leaves, roots, fungus. Roots twist themselves into weird shapes
that look like insects and snakes. Brown mottled frogs hide on the forest
litter. And algae grows in the sloth's fur.

We spend the next day cutting a trail up to Hector's shelter, the newly
acquired RIC property, so that the biologists coming next week will be able
to set their traps.

According to Juan, the area is called Riconda or "deep corner." "Assas-
sins roost" according to Jose.

"You don't like Riconda?" asks Juan.

"Riconda? What's that?" asks Jose.

"That's what people around here refer to it."

"Riconda, I never heard anyone say that," says Jose.

After hacking along a flat area, we begin working uphill. Soon we are
cut off from the river by a steep embankment and can only continue up.
Halfway up the hill Jose stops.

"Hey, uh, we're going uphill here, Juan. I don't know that we want to
be going uphill. Know what I mean, Juan?" Jose shrugs his shoulders and
waves his machete around.

"You know these biologists are going to be carrying these traps around.
They're not going to want to be going uphill now. I just wanted to get from
point A to point B in the simplest way possible, and then you just head

straight up the hill here."

"I guess I made a mistake," says Juan charging up the hill swinging his machete.

"You know maybe you're getting tired, swinging that machete around; you're not looking where you're going. Look, we're just now to the matapalo. I just want to make a nice easy trail from my place, you know what I mean, Juan?"

"You want to go back?"

"Oh, it's too late, *now*." Jose swings at an overhanging vine.

On the summer solstice a near full moon hangs over the banana field. Mars and Venus circle around each other. Jupiter sneaks up from below. Orange blinking eyes of fireflies float over the rotting stumps. I lean against a moss covered log and watch the quick shadows of bats dart among the bananas seeking the ripe fruit. In the buttress of a tree glows a four inch tube of green light. I bend down—*What if it's a snake?*—I straighten up and turn on my flashlight. *Yup, something's glowing.* One of the roots glows a pale green. *Glowing roots, very weird.*

After some deliberation I venture into the jungle. The trees close in becoming black shapes. The sounds of the river, frogs, insects, bats, and tree rodents reverberate through the darkness. Tiny red points of light watch me from above. I resist the urge to turn on the flashlight. I walk slowly, my feet feeling the roots along the path. Coming across a dry creek bed I find a rock and sit in the dark and listen to the night noises. I try telling myself I should go farther into the forest, yet something holds me back. Spirits seem to be about tonight.

Another sunny morning after a rainy night. My last day in Los Cedros, and I hope I see some animals. I'm getting tired of vegetable matter. Sitting in the warm tropical sun, a butterfly alights on my ankle. The sun's so bright I can see the shadows of the butterfly's antennae against my skin. Do butterflies spread their wings like vultures to warm up in the morning sun? A hummingbird shimmers red and green, flirting with an orange and yellow flower dropping from atop an old stump. A bright green parrot darts across the treetops.

One of the rarest and most spectacular inhabitants of the tropics, the Golden-headed Quetzal, alights on a tall snag behind camp. Roger Tory Peterson called the quetzal, "The most spectacular bird in the New World." This technicolor bird sports a bright yellow beak, an iridescent green head and shoulder, a deep scarlet breast and back, and a long (fourteen inch) black tail. Juan and I sit captivated, watching the legendary bird. Sacred to the Maya, the quetzal represented freedom. Now however, deforestation throughout the tropics threatens the bird's survival.

Juan and I excitedly pass the binoculars back and forth.

"I've never seen anything like it," says Juan.

Jose, wandering over to see what all the fuss is about, says, "You've never seen those before, Juan? They're all around here."

The quetzal perches on the snag for a long time, turning its head displaying a proud profile. Then like a prehistoric fantasy creature, it lifts its black and red wings and floats down into the cloud forest out of sight.

I lie in the hammock watching the rain drip as the afternoon descends. Juan comes back from the outhouse and says, "I put the toilet paper under the roof so it won't get soggy."

Jose glances up. "We need fucking windows in the shithouse. We wouldn't have this problem if we had windows in the shithouse, Juan."

"It's a whole lot easier to stick the toilet paper under the roof," Juan says.

The BBC has come on, so quiet time is over. Juan's building a bookshelf and seems quite capable, measuring and planing and leveling, yet Jose has to inspect every step.

"You're going to put this here. I thought we'd have an open bookcase, Juan."

"Okay. I use this and cut a notch out of it," Juan says holding up a 1x2 as a shelf support. "Or I could nail it," he says turning it sideways.

"I think nailing it would be more effective," says Jose.

As Juan begins to nail another support Jose looks over.

"Three nails Juan? You don't need three nails. Just use two. Three nails—you'll split the wood."

I want to ask Juan why he puts up with Jose's abuse when we leave the next morning for Sanjuangal, but we end up talking about the CIA most of the way.

"The CIA invented crack you know, " Juan tells me.

"How do you figure?"

"The CIA is the biggest drug dealer in the U.S. right?"

I have read enough issues of Utne Reader and Mother Jones to recognize the probability of this. "Well I don't know if they actually deal, but they're certainly involved in cocaine trafficking."

"Yeah, okay. So where do you find crack? In black ghettos. It's a shitty drug. It makes you feel shitty. Rich white kids won't touch it. So the CIA comes up with a cheap, shitty drug to keep the black community down. They're all killing each other and totally divided, man."

"Keeps them from getting pissed and having a revolution?"

"You know it, man."

I don't know if the CIA is really behind the crack epidemic, but it's certainly plausible and that's just as scary as if it were true.

We stop at Maria Ellena's, and this time she has warm beer.

Without Jose to dispute everything, Juan's on a roll. "You know when they elected ugly Nixon, I was really surprised. But I figured it was a fluke. Then they re-elected him, I just didn't understand, but they nailed him so I figured okay, that's over. But then they went and elected Reagan, and I was dumbfounded, just couldn't figure it and when they re-elected <u>him</u>! Well, I just didn't know what to think. Then they go and elect Bush, the head of the secret police for chrissakes. I don't think anything can surprise me now."

"You know, I've spent most of my life under Nixon, Reagan and Bush," I say.

"I remember when I was little, must have been five or six, my mom caught me in a lie. She took me aside and said, 'Don't you lie. You don't want to grow up like that man, Nixon, do you?'"

This was my first recollection or right and wrong. The model of immorality held before me was the President of the United States! In civics class we learned about democracy and covered our heads in the hallway in civil defense drills.

"The Soviet Union's overextended. There's too many little countries. It's silly to worry about them, the whole thing will fall apart if they just leave it alone," my mom said in the early 70's.

In sixth grade, Nixon fell. Mom was vindicated. Things almost looked up there in the mid 70's with Jimmy Carter, solar energy, clean air and water, human rights. All gutted by Reagan/Bush returning us to imperialism and business as usual.

I was born just before Kennedy was shot (by the CIA?). I grew up in the shadow of Vietnam and Johnson. Nixon took me to high school. My adult life spent under Reagan/Bush. Why should I have any confidence in American Democracy? The CIA behind the crack epidemic? Why not?

We reach Don Pepe's just as buckets of rain drop from the sky. As we arrive at the road to town, Juan stops by the little store "to wait for Gracilla coming in on the bus." I had been warned and had seen enough of his alcoholism to know that he would be there a long time and I didn't want to be around. Accepting his lame excuse, I walk into town. I plop my soggy self down on the wooden bench at the Sanjuangal "Inn."

Three boys and a girl sit at a table doing their homework by lantern. One of the boys makes a paper hat. I show them how to make paper airplanes, and soon we are all winging paper airplanes about the room. As he picks up his waterlogged plane, one of the boys, about seven, asks me where I'm from. "*Los Estados Unidos,*" I reply.

"Why does the United States blow up people's houses?" he asks.

I shrug and stare into my beer.

Inti Raymi, the
Inca Festival of the Sun

During the neolithic age, mankind made gigantic strides without the help of writing; with writing the historic civilizations of the west stagnated for a long time.

The only phenomenon with which writing has been concomitant is the creation of cities and empires, that is the integration of large numbers of individuals into a political system and their grading into castes and classes.

My hypothesis, if correct, would oblige us to recognize the fact that the primary function of written communication is to facilitate slavery. —Claude Levi-Strauss

Back in Quito I discover our departure for the Huaorani territory is delayed until next week. Ali, a sharp dresser--his long greying hair offsetting a Mexican style vest--arrives from the United States bringing desperately needed funds for RIC. He procured the thousand dollar donation that Jose has already spent. Ali smudges himself with sage in his upstairs apartment in Quito, lighting the herbal bundle on the electric stove, and tells me about the RIC permaculture project. I get the sense that permaculture is a type of organized organic agriculture.

Sparrow shares this apartment with Ali and displays a couple of Huaorani blowguns mounted on the wall like crossed swords. Three Huaorani crowns made from toucan and macaw feathers hang from another wall.

"Ever shot a blowgun?" Sparrow asks.

"Nope," I laugh.

"Wanna try it?"

"Sure, why not?"

Sparrow takes down the blowguns and hands me one of the hollow seven foot pieces of wood. Holding it straight out in front of my face feels clumsy.

"It works a lot better when you point it straight up toward the trees, like you're shooting a monkey," Sparrow says.

But the ceiling is too low for that. So we set up a pillow against the far wall. Sparrow takes down a bamboo quiver, pulls out an incense thin dart, twists a bit of kapok cotton on the end and puts it in the blowgun. The kapok seals the tube so pressure can build up behind the dart. He lifts the blowgun to his mouth, gives a quick puff and the dart instantly sticks into the pillow.

"Wow."

"Give it a try."

He twists the kapok on a dart for me. I drop it in the tube, lift the awkward device to my mouth and blow hard as I can. The dart hits the floor.

"How do you aim this thing?" I ask.

"Just look where you want it to go and give a quick puff. Don't blow so hard."

I do as he says and the dart hits the pillow next to his.

"It's pretty easy," Sparrow adds.

The Huaorani dip the tips of the darts in curare poison to kill monkeys and birds, their main sources of protein.

Inti Raymi, the ancient Inca festival of the sun, begins this weekend. Santiago Morales, a representative of the local indigenous federation, invites us to Cayambe, a village at the base of the 19,160 foot Cayambe volcano just north of Quito, for the festival.

Britta and I join Ali and Jeff, the RIC permaculture project manager, in Cayambe on Saturday morning. Santiago and Jeff have spent the past few months working with thirty indigenous communities near Cayambe setting up South America's first permaculture project.

Large haciendas and corporate farms, which produce dairy products and flowers for export, control the best agricultural lands in the Cayambe valley, consigning the Quichua to the highlands. The permaculture communities are among the poorest, lacking basic services such as potable water, electricity, phones, and health services.

Ali has trouble with breakfast in Cayambe. We try a place Jeff knows. Ali walks in and says *"Buenas dias,"* and the woman behind the counter asks him what he wants, so he walks out.

"She didn't even say *'buenas dias.'* Everyone in this county says *'buenas dias'* when you say *'buenas dias.'* I don't want to eat at a place with someone so fucking rude," he says, disgusted.

Ali doesn't speak Spanish, so he's rather sensitive if things don't go quite right.

The bakery nearby doesn't have coffee. There are no tables at the next place, so that won't do.

Finally we find a place with tables and coffee, (well, *esencia*) but no bread. Britta runs back to the bakery.

Ali says that people in the United States are so tied to the market production of food that if the petroleum infrastructure collapsed, people would starve after exhausting the three day supply of food in grocery stores. Both Britta and I come from rural families and quickly point out the pantry concept.

Ali tells us that the United States is the most evil empire that has ever existed. I want to disagree, but I can't come up with anything to refute this.

The festival doesn't begin until tomorrow, so we join Douglas and Marta for a visit to the Cochasqui pyramids, remnants of the mighty Cara culture, the last conquest of the Incas. Prior to the Inca conquest, the Cara had organized most of present day Ecuador into a loose confederation of villages. Little is know about Ecuador's pre-Inca civilizations because the Inca occupation, while short-lived, was extremely intensively imposed Inca structures, customs and even language on native peoples. "The Incas instinctively adopted many of the most successful devices of colonial and totalitarian regimes," writes John Hemming.

Practicing a policy of displacement of troublesome conquered subjects, the Incas moved the Otavaleños, originally from Lake Titicaca in present day Bolivia, over a thousand miles from their homeland, and dispersed the Cara throughout the empire. The Incas also united all groups under a common language, Quechua. Learning Quechua was compulsory and parents were punished for failing to teach it to their children. In the highlands of Ecuador, Quechua evolved into a distinct dialect, Quichua.

Following the Spanish conquest, disease, culture shock, a chaotic administration, famine and exploitation decimated the indigenous population during the sixteenth century. By the 1700's the Cara language, like many others in the Andes, completely died out, replaced by Quichua.

Furthermore, Spanish historians made little effort to discriminate between the Inca and earlier cultures, and archaeologists thus far have concentrated on Peru, ignoring Ecuador's preColumbian history.

What is known is that the Cara offered the fiercest resistance the Incas encountered during their empire, successfully resisting occupation for seventeen years. The Inca war ended with the marriage of the Cara princess Paccha and the Inca Huayna Capac. Their son was Atahualpa.

This marriage did not pacify everyone, however. A Cara captain named Pinta continued guerilla warfare by hiding out in the forests with a thousand men. Huayna Capac finally captured Pinta, who proved no less troublesome in captivity. Weary of Pinta's resistance, Huayna Capac let Pinta starve and had a drum made from his skin to be played at Cuzco for Inti Raymi.

According to Cara, legend a man descended from the Cayambe volcano and joined with the daughter of corn who gave birth to two sons, Cayambi and Caranqui, who were instructed to populate the two areas named after them. These two communities formed an alliance, giving rise to the Cara culture.

It begins to rain as soon as we arrive at Cochasqui, a few miles from Cayambe. We hang around the museum and look at pots and lithic scrapers until the rain finally lets up a little, and we follow our private guide. (We are the only tourists who want to see the pyramids.)

Up the hill stands a wooden Cochasqui cross—the cross beam halfway up the center pole, indicating the four cardinal points. A three tiered stone base supports the cross. The guide tells us the first tier represents the state, the second the community, and the third the family.

At the pyramids they performed human sacrifices. I suppose individual sacrifices make symbolic sense if family, community and state are the building blocks of your cross.

On the other hand, the Constitution and mythology of the United States stress the importance of the individual. The State appeals to our unfulfilled sense of community in the guise of patriotism. "America" becomes our smallest group identity made possible only though modern mass media. This is the origin of the enormous strength and solidarity of the United States. Television and commercialism maintain our ponderous American identity using Kmart, McDonalds, and Teenage Ninja Mutant Turtles as universal American Icons.

While we walk in the rain I ask Jeff, "So what exactly is permaculture?

What sort of project is this?"

Jeff talks of the failure of the "Green Revolution" and international "development" projects. RIC proposes a small scale, long term approach by working with the local indigenous communities and organizers like Santiago.

Jeff gives a couple examples by way of explanation: using chickens to churn the soil as a biological rake, running pigs through orchards feeding off rotten fruit. A healthy, sustainable community without pesticides, petroleum or monocrops is the goal.

Jeff expresses his challenge, "When I was in Mexico, the Peace Corps showed the farmers a video on reforestation. It showed people planting small trees, and then the next scene showed a forest. They didn't get it. They didn't understand the time sequence; they didn't make the connection between one scene and another. People not used to T.V. or movies aren't going to understand. It's beyond their experience. Trees don't grow in the space of a few minutes; they know that.

"So I've got to figure out how to teach them to build a greenhouse. The Peace Corps gets people involved in these projects. They pay them, in one form or another, so they do it until the Peace Corps person leaves. They don't see the reason behind the project, just the immediate gain. I've got to figure out how to make this project theirs, so they understand the rationale behind it. Some things make sense, like holding the land in common. There's a real sense of community. These people have lived here for generations. They all have the same interests, hobbies, concerns and lifestyle. The hats everyone wears identify which group they belong to."

In so much of Latin America, the self is an extension of the community. A "collective self" emerges, a concept we can never fully understand. Even in spoken language, "we" as community and "I" as self intermingle and become obscured.

If a community can be extended to include the living and nonliving environment, perhaps we can begin to understand what happens to a people when the forests are cut down and the land plowed under. I wonder if we are ready to admit the destruction of place also destroys the soul of a people. Are we willing to take responsibility for this?

We need to view ourselves in context. We can't afford to delude ourselves into thinking that by buying Ben and Jerry's Rainforest Crunch or dropping condoms out of airplanes, we've solved the problem.

Past the cross stand a couple of reconstructed Cochasqui houses and vegetable gardens. Although small and dark, the house looks quite inhabitable. I'm always amazed at how comfortable pre-industrial cultures seem to live. Part of the perpetuation of the American industrial myth is that our lives are better than our ancestors, that our society is the most advanced, the most egalitarian the planet has ever witnessed. The corporate state depends upon the propagation of this myth. Imagine what would happen if we stopped believing it.

It's been long argued that agriculture gave rise to high civilizations with the subsequent increase in leisure time. However, the people with the most time on their hands are hunter/gatherers. More likely, civilizations grew from the centralization of power, and agriculture resulted from the need to keep large segments of the population busy while a few could sit back and reap the benefits. This is not possible under an egalitarian hunter/gatherer system.

The Huaorani have no writing, no status, no class, no laws. Their language contains no numbers above ten. By no means does this suggest their language is any less complex than our own. We base our notions of the primitive solely on technology, yet we have little regard for the technology of the sacred.

Traditionally, our image of a culture's sophistication originates from the quality and impressiveness of their stone monoliths, which immediately suggests subordination under a stratified and authoritarian culture.

Indeed, the Incas provided a welfare state without private property and money. However their society was possible only through extreme class distinctions.

In *Stone Age Economics*, Marshall Sahlins argues that hunter/gatherers have *chosen* their life-styles—basing their economies on the under use of resources. Producing a surplus would lead to population growth, decreased leisure time and a hierarchical society. But is it indeed possible in the burgeoning twentieth century for the Huaorani to freely *choose*?

From under his poncho, Douglas produces six flutes—preColumbian replicas. You blow through a hole in the clay pot-like figures to produce a high pitched whine. An artisan in Albuquerque studied the original flute and made these to exact specifications. The tone depends upon precise dimensions of the inner chambers.

The six flutes are supposed to stop the degradation of the earth when you play at the sacred site on the Solstice. Plus, Jupiter, Venus, and Mars are aligned, and it's a full moon. The solar eclipse is next week. What better celestial timing?

Sitting in an ancient Cochasqui dwelling, the sharp circling tones of the flutes pulls us into the past as it recedes from us. We search backward for a glimpse of sense, for lost connection, a primeval paradise, trying to transcend knowledge and lift ourselves out of our daily pessimism. Unfortunately, the ancients are staring back to the dreamtime when condors married humans.

We follow the guide down to the pyramids, large, flat-topped grassy knolls. Llamas graze on the tall grass over an obviously constructed topography. One of the pyramids is partially excavated. Cochasqui doesn't have an archeologist. The pay is $80 per month, and they can't find anyone who will work for that. Along the top of the pyramid two long troughs line up with Cayambe and Pinchincha. Nearby another trough points to Cotopaxi. Three stone posts stand in line with the troughs to mark the passing of the sun as a calendar. The pyramids are constructed of great blocks of mud as are many of the old walls in Cayambe.

We can see the entire valley, all the way back to Quito and not one native tree in sight (just a few eucalyptus) in an area once covered with dense forest. Ali and Douglas bemoan the loss of forest, bitching about the "bloody Spanish" and campesinos grazing their sheep.

This bitterness I've found among so many environmentalists is disheartening. Bitterness and frustration are certainly understandable when fighting against corporate-industrial momentum. We may not see a fundamental change in our lifetimes; however as Edward Abbey often said, it's important to be a "halfhearted fanatic, a part-time crusader," otherwise you risk losing your humanity.

Am I subverting their efforts by questioning this environmental evangelicalism? If you stop to examine your motives, does that weaken your resolve? Or is there just no time for questions when two to three species vanish every day from the rainforest?

When I hear statistics like this, I find it so distressing that instead of motivating me to action, I feel sad, condemned. It seems I can only get motivated to effect change with me, with what I'm doing, otherwise it's too overwhelming. I always thought I've had some flaw because I couldn't think globally.

I think I was about seven when my best friend told me about "the bomb." "It could blow up the whole world," he said. I didn't believe him. I mean, where would it come from? I pictured a bunch of B-52's flying over the earth and dropping a big bomb. Then where would they go? I still have trouble believing we can *blow up* the whole world. I just can't see it. I have this problem with scale.

These small RIC projects, like creating a bioreserve in Los Cedros, and building a community house for the Huaorani, are on a human scale. Preserving the rainforest begins in the highlands, helping the people who have been pushed off their land build a sustainable future, so they don't have to keep encroaching upon wild areas. Maybe it won't make any difference, maybe the hole in the ozone will fry us anyway. But planting vegetables, building solar cookers and ecological restoration is something I can fathom.

"So what exactly is permaculture?" I ask as we head back to town. Jeff tells me to check out Bill Mollison.

"He's a fucking genius," Ali adds.

Bill Mollison, founder of the Institute of Permaculture, defines permaculture as "the conscious design and maintenance of agriculturally productive ecosystems which have the diversity, stability and resilience of natural ecosystems. It is the harmonious integration of landscape and people, providing their food, energy, shelter and other material and nonmaterial needs in a sustainable way. Without permanent agriculture there is no possibility of a stable social order.

The philosophy behind permaculture is one of working with, rather than against nature; of protracted and thoughtful observation rather than protracted and thoughtless action; of looking at systems in all their functions, rather than asking only one yield of them; and of allowing systems to demonstrate their own evolutions."

For the permaculture project, RIC has rented a house in Cayambe. Jeff needs a broom for the house. Britta and I join him for a search that evening. Jeff stops and asks people in the streets where he can buy a broom. We are finally pointed to a corner shop. Three men stand inside getting a head start on the festival, passing around a bottle of rum. Jeff makes a slow gaze of the shop, before talking with the men about the upcoming fiesta. Eventually he gets around to inquiring about a broom. The store owner hands him an ordinary straw broom. He sights it like a pool cue, hefts it in each hand to check the weight, runs a test sweep of the shop.

"Let's see another," he asks the owner.

Everyone laughs, and a series of jokes that I don't get follow the bottle of rum as they pass it around. An hour later, we finally leave the shop. I'm beginning to appreciate another approach, one of engaging people on an everyday basis. Jeff hardly appears as Zen master, but it seems he regards his daily life as practice.

As we walk through the night time streets of Cayambe, Santiago pulls up and asks us to help him load some chicha for the festival. We pile into his Landcruiser and drive out of town to a mud and tile roof house with no electricity. Three fires inside heat huge bubbling cauldrons. A woman lit only by the glow of the firelight pours water into one of the pots. Sacks of potatoes lie lumped in the corner, a barrel of cooked corn kernels sits in the middle of the room. A girl of four in traditional clothes, even hat, sits on her sister's lap next to the fire. A man dishes out a cup of fresh chicha, a slightly alcoholic drink made from corn, potatoes, sugar, and of course, yuca. The first round of chicha follows a ritual. The cup is offered and you're supposed to quaff it all at once, then it's refilled for the next person. It's warm, thick and very nourishing and goes down easy.

A festive atmosphere fills the plaza on the morning of Inti Raymi. Vendors set up booths, people stroll through the park. "Inti Raymi," the loudspeaker from the museum announces between sporadic bursts of native flutes, drums and guitars. This is the first time in 500 years the ancient festival of the sun will be held at the Temple of the Sun. Since the arrival of the Spanish missionaries, not far behind the conquistadors, Inti Raymi has been celebrated under the veil of the festival of San Pedro. Every year during the village/church celebration of San Pedro, the indigenous people from the highlands come and do a dance around the plaza and go home and get drunk.

This year plans were laid to celebrate Inti Raymi itself. The village, however, decided to cancel Inti Raymi because of "cholera." So, Pablo of the museum and Santiago took it upon themselves to organize Inti Raymi at the Temple of the Sun overlooking the town. They ran into numerous roadblocks by government officials afraid indigenous activity would result in an uprising. Finally two days before the festival they secured the necessary permits. Armored vehicles and soldiers stand by. Just in case.

Santiago invites us in the museum for coffee. The museum is teeming with campesinos. Beaming, Santiago waves his hand at the people crowding around the displays of broken pots and dusty dioramas.

"None of these people have ever been in here. This museum holds their culture. Before, Inti Raymi was just an excuse to get drunk. Now they celebrate their heritage," he says.

As well as the sacred festival of the sun and harvest, Inti Raymi was also a war ritual and a rite of passage for young men entering adulthood. It served to maintain tradition and a sense of community. The festival preceded the Inca occupation by hundreds of years. However, the name "Inti Raymi" was imposed by the Inca overculture which also celebrated the sun on the solstice.

The women, descended from corn, were the keepers of cultural values and knowledge, thus responsible for teaching and passing knowledge on to the next generation. They were also responsible for food and drink, signified by the making of chicha.

Since it's both a community and religious festival, the participants must prepare physically and psychologically. At sacred sites they receive baths of purification.

It has taken a conscious effort on the part of an few educated and dedicated people to pull Inti Raymi out of the drunken party to which it had deteriorated over the years and reestablish a heritage by letting the people know the importance of these rituals.

At ten o'clock the marching band strikes up an off-key, halfhearted funeral march. A marching drum leads the slow procession followed by old men blowing squawky notes on dented brass trumpets; a few clarinets add a high pitch and then San Pedro comes out of the pale blue crumbling church mounted on his throne and borne on the shoulders of four men. People take off their hats as he passes. Others slowly move forward to pin money on the wooden figure. Britta asks a man in a car why they pin money on San Pedro.

"So the priest can buy cigarettes," he replies.

The procession shuffles slowly around the plaza and they take San Pedro back into his cubicle for another year.

By noon I notice a small group gathering at the Temple of the Sun above town. I've lost everyone else in the crowd, so I wander up. A couple blocks from the plaza, next to the cemetery, opens an old stone portal, made from the same blocks as the pyramids at Cochasqui. Walking up the narrow road with stone walls rising ten feet on either side, I hear shouts and singing behind me. A troop of brightly clad campesinos celebrate their way up the trail. Horses and riders and banners and men in masks and guitars and clowns and women in bright green and fuchsia skirts and hundreds of hats all flood toward me. There's nowhere to go, so I press against the wall but get swept along in the procession and carried up the road winding up the pyramid ramp.

Looking back toward town I see a river of people flowing through the streets, up the old road out of town and bottlenecked at the ramp of the pyramid. For over an hour people stream up to the Temple of the Sun.

The parade marches around the perimeter of the pyramid, which the preceding centuries have reduced to a flat knoll, stopping occasionally to dance. After the circumnavigation they break into groups, each indigenous community performing their own dance. Some groups are large and colorful. Others are obviously quite poor, like those communities which will participate in the permaculture project.

Three to five masked men play guitars and occasionally a flute. All the men playing an instrument have their faces covered somehow. Those without masks wear bandanas and sunglasses.

The masks, dubbed "Masques del Diablo" (masks of the devil) by the Spanish, are made of brightly colored cloth with a face (eyes, nose and mouth holes) cut into both front and back. Floppy fingers of cloth protrude from the top, perhaps portraying rays of the sun. I ask a number of people about the masks, but no one, including those wearing them, seem to know what they represent. Santiago suggests they might signify the sun and moon.

In a tight circle around the men, the women, age 12-70, shuffle-dance singing Spanish and Quichua songs. The dances simulate the rotation and cycles of Pacha Mama, (literally "mother earth") says Santiago. The women dress in their finest traditional clothes, pleated skirts of bright fuchsia, green, or teal with gold embroidered trim. Bright gold beads shine against their frilled blouses. The beads used to be real gold until a few years ago when gold dealers showed up and bought everyone's gold. Now the beads are painted glass imported from Japan. The dresses are imported from Iran, and the white frilled blouses come from Pakistan.

And of course, everyone wears their best hats. Each community sports its own type of hat. One community's dancers all wear dark green bowlers with a peacock feather. Eduardo Galeano writes of these hats prevalent throughout the Andes, "Originally they were like cattle brands, compulsory disguises that helped each Spanish master recognize the Indians he owned. As time passed, communities began to deck out their headgear with their own stamps of pride, symbols of joy: stars and little moons of silver, colored feathers, glass beads, paper flowers, crowns of corn . . ."

Two of the soldiers, sabers slapping against their polished knee-high boots, apparently don't take the possibility of uprising too seriously, and appear to be having a great time.

Everyone passes around homemade chicha in Coke bottles or plastic jugs. As they drink more and more, the dances get slower and slower, and it becomes difficult to tell participant from spectator. The crowd merges with the dancers. I soon find myself holding a brightly painted staff with a dead parrot nailed to the top. Caught in the crowd, we march and sing our way down the ramp and up the hill to the house of the previous night. The courtyard is filled with men, guitars, women, dresses, and children. Little girls play Ecuabally in the street holding a string above their heads as a net, lowering it when a car passes. Inside the house we are served up a plastic bag of steaming corn and potatoes.

By evening, bonfires of old tires burn in the streets, People stand around inhaling the fragrant smoke. Her radio blaring traditional music, an old woman, who obviously indulged in too much chicha, dances in the street with her small black dog. A toothless smile on her face.

Everyone else left for Quito hours ago. Jeff and I catch the last bus out of Cayambe. Costumed figures appear out of nowhere dancing down the highway lit by the bus headlights. Masques del Diablo stare at us through the pouring rain and disappear back into the night.

Steel Bars and Concrete Walls

When the tragedy of the world market no longer dominates our existence, unexpected gradations of being in love with being here will emerge. —Walter Lowenfels

Let me say, with the risk of appearing ridiculous, that the true revolutionary is guided by strong feelings of love. It is impossible to think of a true revolutionary without this quality. —Che Guevara

After three months I'm just beginning to scratch the surface, and as I peel back the skin of Ecuador, I get frightened. My bubble feels fragile. Complete immersion—I'm not sure I really want to cross that zone of comfort. I'm afraid of drowning. I feel I'm spending far too much time hanging out with other gringos, but it's so easy—we share a similar fate.

The sale of Hector's land goes smoothly. Two biologists from UCLA arrive to conduct a mammal study of Los Cedros. They will collect baseline data and determine the population of the endangered Brown-headed Spider Monkey.

Unfortunately, they were unable to procure mist nets with which to capture bats. Their small mammal traps shipped by airfreight are still in

Miami. The other traps sit at customs because of a minor paperwork technicality. The biologists are frantic as they only have a few weeks to do the study. Finally the traps are released, and all is set for their departure to Los Cedros. Everyone at RIC is excited because the biologists were able to raise $6000 to purchase additional lands. It looks as if the Los Cedros project is taking off.

Two young men, Nantohue Coba and Moi Enomenga Nantohue, the president and vice president of ONHAE (The Organization of Huaorani People of the Ecuadorian Amazon) are camped out on the living room floor of the RIC house. I spend the morning with them trying to learn Huaorani. "Huaorani," it turns out, means "one person—many people." Coba wants to learn English so we exchange languages in the mutually understood Spanish. My brain gets rather muddled at times. Not surprisingly, Huaorani is like nothing I've ever heard. In fact, it belongs to no other language group in the Amazon. It's a fun language; it even sounds like the jungle. For example, "How are you?" translates, "*Emano imi*," and "I want to eat fish," becomes "*Boto ponemopa quenquin yeye.*"

The next day Jose shows up shaking his head. The biologists left the $6000 in cash they brought in their hotel room while they went to dinner. When they returned it was missing. The biologists verge on breakdown; everyone else, however, takes it in stride. Even I know better than to leave cash in a hotel room.

The day before we are to leave for Huaorani territory I start to feel ill. Douglas comes in and wakes me at five in the morning to leave for the Huaorani territory. I haven't felt well for the past couple days and now I know I'm too ill to go. I shake my head. Bitterly disappointed, I explain my condition, a chronic lung infection which puts me out for two weeks to two months.

Douglas shrugs and heads downstairs.

I curse my body. And lack of commitment. *Che also had asthma, but that didn't keep him out of the revolution.*

Xanthe, manager of the Explorer's Club, takes pity on me and provides a back room at the house so I can recuperate and indulge in chicken soup, sleep, and hot baths.

Watching people come into the Club, I begin to wonder if going to a country to climb mountains constitutes a form of colonialism. Is bagging peaks another example of taking, collecting? What's my real reason for being here? Curiosity? Adventure? Has National Geographic festered my imagination with strange and exotic cultures and places, transforming them into curiosities removed from myself so they may be collected to fill some psychic void?

By exoticizing, by trying to fill gaps in otherwise mundane life, are we seeking a shift in our own identity? Are we using Latin America as a spiritual and psychological dumping ground? I should give something back in exchange for taking this experience home. Maybe we can learn to receive instead of taking. Is it possible to have tourism which is engaging? "Ecotourism" purports to do just this. However, I'm immediately suspicious of anything beginning with "eco." All too often ecotourism means river rafting or gawking at naked Indians.

The U.S. State Department warns against traveling in El Salvador. If your hair is long you must be a communist guerrilla and the Government "disappears" you. If your hair is short, you must be CIA and the guerrillas off you. Not only is El Salvador one of the most dangerous places, it also has some of world's best surfing. Surfers travel with impunity, as if swimming trunks with sharks are letters of diplomats.

I wish I could be apolitical, yet I end up dissatisfied and empty. On the other hand, it seems political action demands selfless commitment, and then I feel I can never be selfless enough and end up feeling guilty and dispirited.

Lying in bed, I think back over the past week trying to put events in some sort of context.

Sparrow had given me some ayahuasca, a psychotropic substance made from vines by jungle shamans for transformation, healing and divination. I placed the film canister of brown goo in a corner of my room. It exploded while I was out one day. The film can was turned over, the cap sat across the room, and the ayahuasca lay in a puddle. Powerful medicine.

The whole world shifted that night. A dense fog rolled in from the mountains and suddenly everything seemed strange. Streets I walked every day, a neighborhood I knew, yet nothing looked familiar. I noticed things, patterns I'd never seen before, buildings, cracks in the sidewalk; colors on the signs seemed more vivid. There was such a heightened sense of awareness that I kept thinking I was lost. The ayahuasca escaped into the world. The ayahuasca was loose in Quito and everything was new and different.

A couple days later, Magali, the RIC secretary and recent refugee from Peru, showed me her apartment overlooking a small valley dominated by a huge cathedral. A cloud formed a milky bridge across the surrounding hills isolating this little town in the middle of Quito. Cutout prints of Picasso and Gauguin decorated the whitewashed walls of her apartment.

She asked if I'd like to read some radio plays she was writing. I sat at her desk under a bare light bulb reading the plays she punches out on a cheap manual typewriter. Magali's radio plays all contain environmental themes, and the trees and worms talk. The one I read was about a *brujo* who bad-mouths the eucalyptus trees, so pervasive throughout the Andes. The spirit of the eucalyptus comes and asks why. So the brujo takes the spirit into the future when eucalyptus dominate the landscape. A eucalyptus is crying because there's nothing but other eucalyptus. All the other trees are long gone.

The centuries of firewood gathering have deforested the Andes, which are now bare except for eucalyptus. Introduced from Australia, the eucalyptus grow rapidly and can be cut down sooner for firewood than the native pines.

Magali made fresh-squeezed orange juice as the evening mists rolled off the lichen covered red tile roofs below. She told me of a small mountain town in Peru where Sendero Luminoso, or Shining Path, which has been compared to both Mao's cultural revolution and Pol Pot, came and killed the mayor and told the hated wealthy landowning family to leave or be killed. They left. Sendero then distributed the land and livestock to the villagers in exchange for their commitment to the movement. So when Sendero needs soldiers they will come and take the men from the village. If you refuse the "gift" they tell you to leave. Over the past ten years "The People's War" has left 25,000 dead in Peru. The deaths are not only from Sendero; the government security forces are equally brutal. The revolution is going to get even bloodier.

Recent reports indicate Sendero has public support and strength equal to the military. Peru is a country divided. Those districts not under military rule are under Sendero control. Sendero's popularity is almost understandable given the living conditions of Peru's campesinos and the failure of land reforms. Sendero presents itself as a real alternative.

Campesina women, who have suffered the most over the years and have long been excluded from established politics and ignored in reform movements, find the movement appealing. In fact, many Sendero leaders are women. Arms give Senderista women respect and authority previously unknown to them.

In typical takeovers of villages, Sendero ousts the male dominated municipal structures, replacing them with "people's committees" where women are able to participate and often dominate, implementing more equitable social structures. The people's committee redistributes land, promotes collective agriculture, provides education for all, and reintegrates ancient rituals.

Sendero takes women's concerns seriously, emphasizing gender equality, and a subsistence economy, of which indigenous women are primarily involved. Women know they will not be raped or abused by a Sendero soldier, nor will they be degraded for being poor, Indian, or female. The darker side of Sendero imposes death penalties for domestic violence, adultery, and rape.

Unafraid of her sadness, Magali looked straight at me while on the verge of tears and continued, "Peru is very beautiful and there are many places of powerful spirits. I will never go back. It's too violent. I went to a meeting and the Sendero were there. I didn't know they were Sendero when I went. But this woman took the mike and said she was Sendero and they tried to take the mike away and all these people stood up and starting saying things and chanting 'Sendero.' It was their faces that frightened me. Their faces were empty, blank. They were like robots, all saying the same thing. They didn't do anything, but I was very scared."

She fell back against the wall, as if saying this took great energy.

Last Saturday afternoon I met Gerard outside the cylindrical modern Casa De Cultura. Gerard told he came down with amoebic dysentery while he was on the coast last week and had to be hospitalized for two days. He thought it was cholera. He seemed to be fully recovered so after condolences, I asked him about the coast.

"Dude, you better be careful. This place is crazy. I was staying near the beach . . ."

"Did you camp out?"

"No way, that's asking for trouble. I went out for a morning walk along the beach. I figured, hey, morning, no problema. This guy in rags comes running up to me and runs by. He's covered in blood. I kept walking and down the beach I found a woman he'd beaten, robbed and raped."

"If I'd been there ten minutes earlier I would have had my head blown off," he said.

Filled with Picasso-esque paintings, the Casa de Cultura served as the contemporary art museum. Unfortunately, all the paintings wore flat battleship grey frames covered with finger smudges. Those near the bottom had a thin film of grime along the lower edge.

The hidden highlight of the museum was a room containing thousands of musical instruments including numerous flutes and drums of Ecuador's indigenous cultures. Next to the drum, the flute is the oldest musical instrument and the exhibit showed variations over thousands of years. Pan pipes alone filled an entire wall. In the middle of the room squatted a huge xylophone from the selva. Varying lengths of bamboo tubes formed the sound chambers and a wooden mallet supplied the percussion. A diversity of shapes and sizes of string instruments lined another wall. Unfortunately, no text accompanied the instruments.

Wandering through the museum, Gerard and I came to a sunny, open room with some bizarre and very ugly sculptures. Gerard and I stood in front of one of the lifeless clay blobs laughing when a Norteamericana approached and asked, "So what do you think," with an effected artistic air. Thinking she may be the perpetrator we couched our comments.

"Uh, well, I don't know that I really understand it. I'm from Montana and mostly see buffalo sculptures," I said.

"Well...." And she went into to a long spiel about the artist's sensitivity and connection with the Earth and Being and free-flow imagination and all.

She worked for the Peace Corps training volunteers. The sculptor was a friend of hers. She reminded us that on the Fourth of July there would be a huge celebration with fireworks on the outskirts of town, put on by the U.S. Embassy. I'd seen signs all over town large newspaper ads for the event.

"Everyone is invited. Of course, you need to show your U.S. passport at the gate to be allowed in," she added.

Gerard related a story from our Dutch friends, Kaes and Marti. It seems they were hitchhiking from a village where they went to investigate a community development project gone awry. They couldn't find any sign of the veterinary clinic that was supposed to have been constructed with the funds. Upon leaving they were picked up by the German veterinarian who was to have staffed the clinic. He said that when he arrived last year, the village had spent all the money on a fiesta. He was so upset that he started poisoning the dogs in town. He confessed that the back of his truck was full of sacks of dead dogs.

Britta stops by the Explorers Club and insists I see a naturopath friend of hers from India who runs a vegetarian restaurant downtown. The herbalist writes me out a prescription for my lungs. She says to eat ten to fifteen oranges every day, one pineapple or papaya for breakfast, yuca or potatoes or rice for lunch, take hot baths in eucalyptus leaves and not to eat any dairy or meat or alcohol. *Ten to fifteen oranges a day?*

Britta leads me in my fevered state to the witch's market to buy eucalyptus leaves. Inside the old warehouse, we wander around among the booths stacked high with various dried leaves, flowers, herbs. They all look like eucalyptus leaves to me. Most of the vendors are gone this late in the day. We finally come upon an old woman hidden among bundles of leaves and bottles and what in my fevered state look like dried lizards and monkey heads. She reaches high up her stacks and fills my arms with bunches of the thin, dried leaves.

Within a week of this treatment, I'm feeling much better and walk over to the RIC house to see how things are going. A white Ford Taurus is parked outside with two men in suits inside. *Oh shit. Something's up.* Jose and Jeff stand in the doorway.

"What's going on?" I ask.

"Welcome to the house of the dead," says Jose.

Ohmygod! Someone's died.

"What! What happened?"

"It's all in the papers, man," says Jose.

"What? What's in the papers?"

"They arrested Douglas, man."

"Why? What for?"

"We don't know," he says and heads upstairs.

"Douglas, Ali, Sparrow and Kevin were taken into custody in Coca by the Army and are being deported," says Jeff.

"But why?"

"That's just it, man, we don't know," calls down Jose.

Xanthe and I pack food, books and Kevin's sleeping bag to bring to the jail. The jail is in the part of town which always seems dark, even at midday. The first three taxis refuse to take us. Finally procuring one, our taxi slides through the narrow streets, surfacing at the top of a hill, an armored island surrounded by decaying colonialism in rush hour despair.

Men in sharp uniforms, their green pant legs tucked neatly inside shiny black calvary boots, mill about. Long sabers dangle from their sides and .45 automatics are strapped under their arms. Some carry automatic rifles. It's difficult to tell whether they are police or soldiers.

An armored car sits in front of the dilapidated colonial building, indistinguishable except for the bars across the windows. The prison guards are unarmed and not exactly in uniform. Guards are the lowest on the scale, one step above prisoners.

The guard at the gate says we can't go in and holds out his hand. Xanthe steps back and says, "He wants us to pay him."

"Okay, how much?" I ask.

"I don't know."

I give him 1500 sucres ($1.50), and he lowers the chain. We walk up some concrete steps and three men in old, green coats stand in the doorway.

"We want to see our friends."

"No, you can't," the guard tells us.

"Why not?"

"You have to wait for approval."

"Okay"

"Do we have to bribe these guys too?" Xanthe asks.

"Sure, why not?"

But the guard lets us through to see the man behind the desk with the big ledger book.

"We want to see our friends, and bring them some things."

"No, you can't. Leave your things here and we'll give them to them," he says.

"No way."

"You can't go in; it's after five," he then informs us.

"What do we do now?" Xanthe asks.

"Wait."

A few minutes later he waves us forward and stamps our hands. We walk through a pale blue gate. Another guard checks my pack, giving it a squeeze.

A man with his shirt unbuttoned halfway down his hairy chest and a massive crucifix around his neck shows us up a flight of dark stairs to a metal gate. Eighty or so middle-aged men stare at us. I can feel Xanthe's apprehension. I wouldn't want to be the only woman in this room. The gate clangs behind us.

Fifteen bunks line the walls of the concrete room. Some men are sleeping. Others are smoking, talking, squatting against the far wall. One man paces back and forth. It's much better than I expected of an Ecuadorian jail. Lying on a couple bunks are four tired looking gringos.

Douglas, Ali, Sparrow, and Kevin are happy to see us, as we dump books, croissants, chocolate, and fruit on their cots. In a fit of poetic irony, I include Philip Agee's Inside the Company.

"I always wanted to read this," Ali says picking up the book.

"The guy next to me is the kick-boxing champ of Ecuador," Kevin says and motions to the next bunk. "He's my friend."

"Everyone's real nice," adds Ali.

Their fellow inmates look after them, bringing coffee in plastic bowls, giving up bunks so they would not have to sleep on the floor, allowing them first place in the chow line. As political prisoners they are the closest thing to celebrities any of these men have had contact with. The five dollars the British Ambassador gave the head prisoner didn't hurt either.

"There's other gringos here. A couple on their honeymoon tried smuggling a couple kilos of coke. Looks like they will be here for fifteen years or so," says Ali.

Between puffs of his cigarette, Douglas explains that the Army is in the not-so-subtle employ of international oil companies to keep the Oriente secure for exploration. The oil companies dislike the idea of independent environmentalists working with indigenous people and had them detained.

I suspect the oil companies prefer environmentalists like Robert Kennedy Jr. of Natural Resources Defence Council (NRDC) and Ted Macdonald of Cultural Survival, who, acting on the assumption that Conoco is the lesser of many evils, met with Conoco officials last winter to discuss petroleum development. NRDC and Cultural Survival were soliciting a $25 million donation from Conoco to establish a foundation for Huaorani community development projects and for scientific research and protection of Yasuni National Park in exchange for not opposing Conoco's leasing activities.

"For reasons that are still unclear, Cultural Survival and NRDC have recently assisted Conoco in rescuing its project, threatening to undermine two years of planning and lobbying on the part of Ecuadorian environmentalist and indigenous groups to fend-off Conoco's development scheme," reports *La Campaña Amazonia por la Vida*, a coalition of thirteen environmental and human rights organizations solidly opposed to petroleum development in Yasuni National Park and the Huaorani Territory.

Kennedy stated in a meeting with Conoco that NRDC accepts the reality that Ecuador will develop its resources and "NRDC believes that it is better to have Conoco do the developing than anyone else." He also stated, "the environmental community is having second thoughts about the wisdom of not dealing with big business."

Amidst charges of environmental imperialism, in a meeting with CONFENIAE, a group of 960 Ecuadorian Amazonian communities, Kennedy emphasized the "inevitability" of petroleum development and expressed his belief that Conoco is "serious about its promises," and susceptible "to our influence."

"So what's going to happen," I ask Douglas.

He shrugs. "Looks like they'll deport us."

Later from Jeff, I get more of the story. What Douglas didn't know was that orders came from the military to get these guys out of the Oriente. A false intelligence report surfaced implicating RIC in "subversive activities" and inciting indigenous uprisings.

The military operates separately from the "democratically elected" government. The Ecuadorian government itself wasn't necessarily interested in the RIC activists and would just as soon oppose the military's efforts.

The military could not actually deport them. So the government, under pressure from a friend of RIC, Tony Muñoz of IREAC, and the British Embassy, finally relented, releasing Douglas, Ali, Sparrow and Kevin without deportation a few days later.

Although none of the activists were British citizens, the British embassy was instrumental in securing their release. The Ambassador pointed out that arresting and holding citizens without charges is a serious human rights violation. From deep inside their midcity fortress, the American Embassy seemed unconcerned. They certainly didn't address any inquiries or return my calls. The incident made front page headlines in the Quito newspapers for two days and went completely unnoticed in the United States.

Riding back from the jail through the crowded nighttime streets of "old town," I gaze out at the people streaming through the streets, stopping for a quick bite at a street stand grill. Campesinos line up at *bodegas* buying candy with their market money from selling pigs and vegetables. I feel like a diplomat in a limo. By what strange quirk am I on this side of the glass, on this side of the bars? It's really a boundary problem. I have weak boundaries; things leak in. Still, I try to keep my world from wobbling too much.

A few days later, Britta invites me to attend a school play that her goddaughter, Consuela, is in. Consuela's father is a security guard in the pleasant middle class neighborhood of Britta's Ecuadorian family. He, his wife and four kids live in the back of one of the larger houses. He makes fifty dollars a month. They can't afford any of the nearby schools, so the children have to go across town to one of the most rundown sections of Quito. Britta sort of "adopted" this family and was honored as the godmother of Consuela.

The family Britta resides with, a few blocks away, lives in a modest house with nice furniture, a color TV and VCR, and a little dog. The father is a doctor. Both son and daughter are in high school. Patricio drives a '71 Chevy Nova, has a Doors poster on his wall and braces on his teeth. Viviana hides in the bathroom so I won't see her in her pajamas.

Britta doesn't know the address of Consuela's school, so we drive around asking people in the neighborhood where they think it might be. The cab driver asks people on the street; I run into a *bodega*; Britta asks at an apartment building. But no one has ever heard of the Juan De Mera School. We drive to another neighborhood and ask around. I think the cab driver would be getting irritated, but he's enjoying the hunt. Somehow we eventually find it and are only fifteen minutes late. Consuela's father greets us at the gate.

We are given seats of honor, folding chairs. Britta videotapes the program to everyone's delight, while Consuela's brother, about three years old, sits on my lap. He's been sick for two weeks, and was in the hospital, but it was too expensive so they had to take him out before finding out what was wrong.

The school girls perform short skits and songs with an institutional shyness which vanishes as soon as the program ends and they are released. They crowd around us wanting to know their names in English and the names of U.S. basketball teams. Then they demand autographs, screeching "*firma me*" sticking out notebooks and hands for us to sign. Classes resume but since there are only four teachers, students have a rotating recess, with one group playing basketball while the teachers conduct the next class. Everyone cheers when anyone on either team makes a basket.

These school girls will live their lives in extreme poverty in an overcrowded city. I have more money in my pocket (fifteen dollars) than their families will see all week. None can afford education beyond this school. When they leave these walls, they are swallowed up by the city, abused by brothers, fathers, husbands, pregnant by sixteen, encased in poverty. They will sell bottles of orange Fanta at small bodegas or lottery tickets on Avenida Amazones; their sons will shine shoes and their daughters will attend a school like this one, if they are fortunate. Their future holds little, if any, hope.

So often we are afraid to touch the magic in the world. Yet we climb mountains and float rivers hoping for a glimpse. Then it comes, all the mystery of the world glistening in the palm of an eight-year-old girl as she takes your hand to play basketball on a small court surrounded by crumbling concrete walls.

EPILOGUE

"Look everyone, I'm back!" I want to yell in the Miami airport, but they're frowning.

I want to grab them and shake them and say, "Do you have any idea how lucky you are? Do you have any idea how lucky you are to even be IN an airport? To have a clean place to shit? How can you possibly be frowning?"

At the espresso and yogurt bar sits a tall, skinny guy with a world peace sign patch on his pack. I notice a *chegria* bag hanging on the back of his stool. Somebody normal I can talk to. So I sit down next to him.

"These spiffy clean aluminum bathrooms are great, but you know, I just can't get used to throwing the toilet paper <u>into</u> the toilet." I say.

"Yeah, I know what you mean, man." He stares into his coffee giving it a swirl. "I know what you mean."

Upon returning to Montana friends asked me, "So how was Ecuador?"

"Um, well, I um...."

This was a difficult question to answer. I couldn't say the expected, "It was great. You should go there." In truth I was unsure of what to make of the whole experience, and I didn't know why.

"Green," was the only answer that truthfully came to mind. So their attention soon drifted to another conversation while I stood there confused. *How <u>was</u> Ecuador?*

I stayed abreast of Conoco's plans for oil development in Ecuador, and in October 1991, a friend, the editor of the Earth First! Journal, handed me a press release in which Conoco announced it was considering canceling its

petroleum plans, withdrawing from the Block 16 lease in the Oriente, cit-
ing opposition by environmental and indigenous groups. However, the
other members of the exploration group planned on pursuing exploration.
Conoco CEO Nicandros stated in the press release, "This was a difficult
decision because it is a good project.... But we simply have more good
projects to do than our capital resources can cover... Conoco Ecuador plans
provide a road map for safe, environmentally responsible projects of this
type." Conoco's withdrawal left the primary interests in the oil exploration
group leasing block 16 as Overseas Petroleum and Investment Corp. of
Taiwan and Maxus Energy Corporation of Texas.

It remained to be seen whether NRDC and Cultural Survival would
continue to work with Conoco's ex-partners, as Conoco CEO Nicandros
said, "I salute those interest groups and individuals who saw the value of a
continuing, constructive dialogue. I urge them to maintain this positive
relationship with the future Block 16 operator and to seek ways to work
with all governments and companies to encourage environmentally responsible development worldwide."

One day I walked into Bill Kittredge's office at the University of Montana and told him I had all this material about Ecuador and I wanted to do
some magazine articles, but I was having a hard time distilling things out. I
had lots of information, but I couldn't isolate it from my own experience.

"If that's the case," he said, "You ought to just write a fucking book."

Going back through my journals, playing and wrestling with the material, I began to understand why seemingly isolated incidents affected me so.
Had I merely left the experience alone, it would decompose into memory
of a grand adventure; I would remember the highs and forget the lows.
However, in the process of interacting with the material and turning over
my mind's compost heap, I finally heard what my subconsciousness was
screaming at me.

Upon returning I found, lodged in the corner of the sugar sack covering my pack, an small onion I'd bought in Vilcabamba. Ecuador would
not stay behind. Not only was Ecuador no longer an unknown banana
republic or a check off of "been there, done that," but it changed me in
ways which I am only now beginning to understand. The awareness received from this visit to Ecuador can never be reciprocated. Surely though,
Ecuador owns me as much as I now own Ecuador.

By becoming part of me, the experience is now mine. I am responsible,
not only for bringing to consciousness an understanding of that experience, but to the conditions and place, the people and land which shaped

that experience.

As of fall 1992, Maxus oil company assumed control of Block 16 and intends on following Conoco's lead, building the road to a cluster of seven well heads. Recent reports indicate the Tangeri group has moved into Block 16.

BIBLIOGRAPHY

Agee, Philip. *Inside the Company: CIA Diary.* New York: Bantam Books, 1975.

Andreas, Carol. "Women at War." *Report on the Americas: Fatal Attraction, Peru's Shining Path.* Volume 24, number 4, 1/91.

Baker, Will. *Backward: An Essay on Indians, Time, and Photography.* Berkeley: North Atlantic Books. 1983.

Bemelmans, Ludwig. *The Donkey Inside.* New York: The Viking Press. 1941.

Berry, Wendell. "Preserving Wildness." *Wilderness.* Spring 1987.

Bierhorst, John. *Black Rainbow: Legends of the Incas and Myths of Ancient Peru.* Toronto: McGraw-Hill Ryerson Ltd. 1976.

Caufield, Catherine. *In the Rainforest.* Chicago: University of Chicago Press. 1984.

Furst, Peter, ed. *Flesh of the Gods.* Praeger Publishers, 1972.

Galeano, Eduardo. *Century of the Wind.* New York: Pantheon Books, 1988.

Gill, Frank, B. *Ornithology.* New York: W.H. Freeman and Company. 1990.

Gilman, Robert. "No Simple Answers." *In Context.* Spring 1992.

Gorriti, Gustavo. "The War of the Philosopher-King." *The New Republic.* June 18, 1990, p15-22.

Greer, Germaine. *Sex and Destiny: The Politics of Human Fertility.* New York: Harper and Row. 1984.

Halsell, Grace. *Los Viejos: Secrets of Long Life from the Sacred Valley.* Emmaus, PA: Rodale Press, Inc. 1976.

Harrison, Paul. *Inside the Third World.* London: Pelican Books. 1987.

Head, Suzanne, and Heinzman, Robert, ed. *Lessons of the Rainforest.* San Francisco: Sierra Club Books, 1990.

Hemming, John. *The Conquest of the Incas.* London: Macmillan. 1970.

Hewett, Edgar, Lee. *Ancient Andean Life.* New York: The Bobbs-Merrill Company. 1939.

Horwich, Robert, H. and Lyon, Jonathan, *A Belizean Rainforest.* Gray Mills, WI: Orangutan Press.

Janzen, Daniel, ed. *Costa Rican Natural History.* Chicago: University of Chicago Press. 1983.

Karsten, Rafael. *The Civilization of the South American Indians.* New York: Alfred A. Knopf. 1926.

Kennedy, Robert, F. Jr. "Amazon Crude." *The Amicus Journal.* Spring 1991.

Kimerling, Judy. *Amazon Crude.* 1991.

Kricher, John, *A Neotropical Companion.* Princeton University Press. 1989.

Man, John. *Jungle Nomads of Ecuador—The Waorani.* Amsterdam: Time-Life Books. 1982.

Maslow, Jonathan Evan, *Bird of Life, Bird of Death*. New York: Dell Publishing Co., Inc. 1986.

Michaux, Henri. *Ecuador: A Travel Journal*. Seattle: University of Washington Press. 1968.

Miller, Tom. *The Panama Hat Trail*. New York: William Morrow and Co., Inc. 1986.

Mollison, Bill. *Permaculture*. Island Press. 1992.

Nichols, John. "A Funny Thing Happened on my Way to the Nobel Prize: I Tripped over my Conscience." March 9, 1988.

Parlow, Anita. "Worlds in Collision." *The Amicus Journal*. Spring 1991.

Rainforest Information Centre. "Permaculture Cayambe—An Integrated Model of Sustainable Agriculture." April, 1991.

Rainforest Information Centre. "Proposal for the Delimitation and Protection of Huaorani Territory." 1990.

Rival, Laura. "Sacred Words and Wild People: Human Rights, Development, Oil and the Huaorani of Amazonian Ecuador." 1991.

Rosenberg, Tina. "Guerrilla Tourism." *The New Republic*. June 18, 1990, p23-25.

Schultes, Richard, Evans, *Plants of the Gods*. McGraw-Hill Book Company. 1979.

Smith, R. G. "Report on Ecuadorian Rainforest." 1991.

Stewart, Julian, ed. *Handbook of South American Indians, Vol. 2*. Smithsonian Institution, Bureau of American Ethnology, bulletin 143. New York: Cooper Square Publishers, Inc. 1963.

Thomsen, Moritz. *Living Poor: A Peace Corps Chronicle*. Seattle: University of Washington Press. 1969.

Von Hagen, Victor Wolfgang. *Ecuador the Unknown.* New York: Oxford University Press. 1940.

Weil, Thomas E. et al. *Area Handbook for Ecuador.* Washington D.C.: U.S. Government Printing Office. 1973.

Whymper, Edward. *Travels Amongst the Great Andes of the Equator.* New York: Charles Scribner's Sons. 1892.